Preparing for
EASTER

Preparing for
EASTER

JAMES L. EVANS

TYNDALE HOUSE PUBLISHERS, INC., WHEATON, ILLINOIS

Library of Congress Cataloging-in-Publication Data

Evans, James L., date
  Preparing for Easter / James L. Evans.
    p. cm.
  ISBN 0-8423-5016-0 (pbk.)
   1. Lent—Prayer-books and devotions—English. 2. Holy Week—Prayer-books and devotions—English. I. Title.
BV85.E93 1993
242.3'4—dc20
                                             93-30563

Printed in the United States of America

00 99 98 97 96 95 94
8   7   6   5   4   3   2   1

For Brenda,
who helped me find my way

CONTENTS

Seventh Week (Holy Week)

Reclaiming the Easter Season

T he foundation of Christianity is the resurrection of Jesus Christ. No one who claims Christ as Savior would dispute that claim. And yet, during the Easter season, at the time of year when Christians have the best opportunity to explore and express the meaning of resurrection, we allow a host of highly questionable symbols to compete for our loyalty.

I am not suggesting that there is anything evil or satanic about the Easter bunny, egg hunts, or candy-filled baskets. These images make up some of our favorite childhood memories. What I am saying is that these symbols are products of our culture and are ultimately contrary to the meaning of resurrection. No matter how hard we may try to baptize them and make them Christian symbols, they retain their powerful connections to nature worship.

Celebrations of the renewal of spring are as old as humanity. Families linked to agriculture paid close attention to the cycle of death and rebirth that takes place in nature year after year. The return of plant life became an important festival for these agrarian people. They depicted their joy over the renewal of the land with symbols of fertility. Some of these include the egg and the rabbit. While it may be true that the renewal of nature may offer hints into the mystery of resurrection (1 Cor. 15:35-38), it can also lead us away from important understandings.

How did these symbols of nature worship become associated with Christianity in the first place? We must remember that for hundreds of years, Christianity existed as a small and relatively new religion in a world filled with ancient religions. As Christianity slowly began to make inroads toward respectability, leaders sought ways to advance the recognition of Christianity as a major religion. One way ancient leaders sought to do this was by tying certain Christian festivals to pagan festivals already in existence.

The first Easter, the day of the resurrection of Jesus, occurred in connection with the Jewish Passover, which occurs on the fifteenth of the Hebrew month Nisan. To this day, people of the Jewish faith celebrate Passover on this date. But notice your own calendar. You will see that Easter and Passover are not on the same day.

Around A.D. 400, bishops in Italy began to recalculate the date of Easter to coincide with the cycle of the spring equinox. A major festival of spring was observed throughout the Roman Empire in connection with this change in the length of days. Christian leaders hoped to unite the celebration of the death and resurrection of Christ with this widely observed holiday. Within a few years this method of calculation became the official way of determining the date of Easter.

I am not suggesting we reopen the case on calculating Easter. I am just making the point that for a long time Easter has been subject to many accommodations resulting from powerful spring observances. Even the word *Easter* reflects this process. The word is an Old English word meaning "dawn." Some scholars think it may be linked to an ancient Teutonic goddess named *Eastre*. This pagan deity was referred to as the "dawn goddess." Her festival time was early spring. The word *Easter* only occurs in the King James Version at Acts 12:4. However, all modern translations render this word *Passover*, which, of course, is the correct translation.

This method of accommodation was probably necessary for the young church to survive in a totally pagan environment. However, the ancient church had one distinct advantage over the modern church in this struggle for identity. In order to assure that Christian believers were able to distinguish clearly between Christian and pagan practices, the entire season preceding Easter was devoted to special instruction and worship emphasis. This period of preparation came to be known as Lent.

Lent is the forty-day period preceding Holy Week, the week just before Easter Sunday. During this forty-day period believers prepare for Easter by reliving, through the whole course of Scripture, God's redemptive history. Lent is a time for renewing commitments to Christ and repenting from acts of disobedience. Lent is also a time to focus on the disciplines of spiritual growth. For forty days, Christians remember the fall of Adam, the call of Abraham, the covenant with Israel, the call of King David. Believers also reflect on the coming kingdom and its hope. Moving closer to Easter, Christians turn their attention to the Suffering Servant—the Messiah.

As Lent comes to an end, Holy Week begins with Palm Sunday, the day Jesus entered Jerusalem, hailed as a king. The remaining days of Holy Week focus on the final events of Jesus' life leading up to the betrayal by Judas and ultimately the Crucifixion.

Christians of old found many ways to visualize and symbolize their observance. Primarily, however, pulpits and homes were adorned with wooden crosses, crowns made of thorns, and candles. By reading selected Scripture every day and reliving God's history that led to the death of Jesus on the cross, Christians are able to fill the renewal of spring with an even deeper meaning—resurrection.

Resurrection is not merely the renewal of life. Resurrection is life out of death. Many evangelical churches in our day realize that culture and society present powerful alternatives to the meaning of Easter. We struggle to know how to assert effectively the distinctive Christian message of new life in Christ. One way many evangelicals are addressing this challenge is by rediscovering Lent and the entire Easter season. This rediscovery is exactly what this book is about.

HOW TO USE THIS WORSHIP GUIDE

The most difficult part of observing Lent for those who are not part of a liturgical church is to figure out when to start. We are accustomed in our evangelical tradition to having only Palm Sunday and Easter Sunday to think about. Lent, however, involves considerably more than just two Sundays. Lent begins on Ash Wednesday—forty-six days before Easter. Unfortunately, just as Easter falls on a different date each year, so does Ash Wednesday. Finding Ash Wednesday is easy enough. Take your calendar for the current year and locate Easter Sunday. Now, count back forty-six days. You should end on a Wednesday—Ash Wednesday (I have listed several years of Ash Wednesday and Easter dates at the end of this introduction).

Ash Wednesday receives its name from the ancient tradition of marking the forehead with ashes in the shape of the cross. As ministers made the sign of the cross on the foreheads of worshipers they would say, "Remember you are dust." It is because we are of the dust of the earth that God must act to redeem us.

Once you have found Ash Wednesday, you are ready to begin Lent. The word *Lent* comes from an old English word meaning "lengthen" and has to do with the lengthening days of spring. The word has come to mean "preparation." The forty-six days of Lent are a time for us to prepare for the crucifixion and resurrection of Jesus. This is where this worship guide begins. The worship guide is divided into seven sections. Each of the first six sections feature worship activities based on traditional Lenten themes. Each week of Lent challenges us to review and renew our covenant faith. The categories we cover are listed below.

1. *From the Dust of the Earth.* This section covers the creation and fall of humankind. This section also reveals God's plan for our redemption—the coming in the flesh of his Son, Jesus Christ.

2. *The Promise to Abraham.* God's first step in redeeming us from our fall was to call Abraham. This section explores the meaning of the promise made to this great man of faith.

3. *The Promise to Israel.* This section recalls the next step God took in our redemption—the covenant with Israel. This covenant included the Ten Commandments.

4. *The Promise to David.* The fourth section puts the spotlight on David. The hoped-for Messiah was seen through the lens of promises made to Israel's greatest king. Eventually, the people of Israel came to believe that the Messiah would be in the likeness of David.

5. *The Promise of the Kingdom of God.* This section will help us understand what it is that God has promised us in his offer to be our King.

6. *The Promise of the Suffering Servant.* This section will focus on Isaiah's vision of the Messiah as a suffering servant king. These powerful poems are among the most beautiful in all of Scripture. This section concludes on Palm Sunday. In the triumphant entry we see Jesus freely accepting the role of the humble servant of God who suffers for his people.

7. *Holy Week.* The seventh section marks the beginning of the last week of Jesus' earthly life. This section climaxes with the Crucifixion and the effort of Pilate to seal the tomb.

The resurrection of Jesus by the power of God brings a dramatic finish to the long history of God's plan to save us. In this book we encourage the use of visual symbols. These are helpful for a number of reasons. First of all, everyone—especially children—more easily remember what they see and hear. One of the goals of this family worship effort is to help children take possession of the Christian story as their own.

Visual symbols also help believers embrace our wider Christian heritage. Traditionally, Lenten celebrations have featured a wooden cross and a crown of thorns. These symbols portray in graphic detail the cost of redemption. They state in clear terms the nature of our Lord's kingship. Jesus was the Suffering Servant King. His throne was a cross, and his crown was of thorns. With these he purchased our release from the power of sin. Resurrection is God's stamp of approval on all Jesus said and did on our behalf.

The use of seven purple candles, as this book encourages, may help visualize the movement through the weeks of Lent toward Easter. Each candle represents one week of Lent, purple being the traditional color for lent. The dark color points to the darkness of sin that sent Jesus to the cross.

During the first week one candle is lit; during the second week two candles, and so on, continuing until Holy Week. As Holy Week begins, worship is started by the lighting of all seven purple candles, followed by extinguishing one candle. The next night seven candles are lit and two candles are extinguished, then three, and so on. On Good Friday, the day of crucifixion, there will only be one candle left burning as the others are extinguished. This gradual elimination of light will help the worshipers see and feel the darkness that gripped the world as the Savior gave his life for us (Matt. 27:45).

Early Easter morning, as closure is brought to your family worship celebration, one large white candle is added to the seven purple candles. These lighted candles symbolize that the light of the world overcame death and the grave.

Each worship activity given here in this book will feature a similar pattern. Directions are given to help you know where you are in Lent (for example, Week 2, Day 2). A Scripture reading and the title for the day's emphasis are listed. A brief description is given of the materials you will need to illustrate the lesson for the day. Instructions will also be reviewed each day concerning the lighting of the candles.

Many of the activities were written on the assumption that they will be done at night. Evening is often the best time for families to worship together. However, you are certainly encouraged to creatively adapt these worship activities to suit the needs of your family.

I am convinced that with just a small amount of dedicated effort all of us can bring a renewed sense of joy and meaning to our celebration of Easter. In a world confused and looking for hope, we can offer God's best remedy—his Son, raised from the dead. Our consistent efforts also will help our own children find their way through the tangled maze of conflicting symbols surrounding Easter. In the long run, that may be the best gift we ever give them.

May the Lord richly bless our efforts to celebrate his gift of life in Jesus Christ.

ASH WEDNESDAY
AND
EASTER DATES

Year	Ash Wednesday	Easter
1994	February 16	April 3
1995	March 1	April 16
1996	February 21	April 7
1997	February 12	March 30
1998	February 25	April 12
1999	February 17	April 4
2000	March 8	April 23

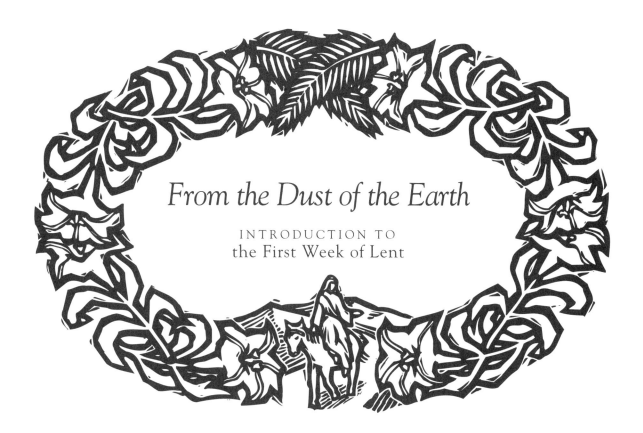

From the Dust of the Earth

INTRODUCTION TO
the First Week of Lent

The book of Genesis teaches that humans were formed from the dust of the earth. We share life with all the rest of creation. Scientists have found, for example, that all of the compounds found throughout the universe exist in the human body. We are part of all we see. And yet we are more.

Genesis also teaches that God breathed into us the breath of life. Our lives are gifts from God. We were given a special place in creation. God invited humans to be his coworkers. In the Garden of Eden where God first created human life, he gave us limits—rules to follow. We did not follow them. As a result, sin entered into the world and spoiled God's perfect plan.

God was not content to simply allow his creation to fail. He took steps immediately to redeem his creation. The Psalmist says, "He does not deal with us according to our sins. . . . For he knows our frame; he remembers that we are dust" (Ps. 103:10, 14).

We begin our journey through Lent at this point of human failure. Our children need to understand this negative potential in them and in all of us. They also need to learn about Jesus Christ, God's remedy for our failure. The next seven days will concentrate on these themes.

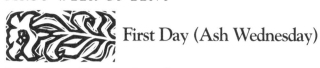 **First Day (Ash Wednesday)**

Light One Purple Candle

"Remember, You Are Dust"

SCRIPTURE
READING

Genesis 2:7; Psalm 103:1-14

MATERIALS
NEEDED

Small amount of dirt and ashes

LESSON

Begin your worship time by briefly explaining what you are trying to accomplish by observing Lent. You might say something like, "Easter is so important for Christians that it deserves more than just one day. We want to get ready for Easter by thinking about all the things that lead up to Easter. We want to spend some special time thinking about all that God has done for us."

Have someone light one candle. Involve children as age and maturity allow. Call on a designated family member to read the two Scripture selections.

DISCUSSION

When the reading is finished, show everyone the dirt. Remind everyone that the Genesis reading said that humans were formed out of the dust of the earth. You might say, "Thinking we are dust might make us feel unimportant. We don't think very highly of dirt. But God does. The psalmist says that because God remembers we are dust (Ps. 103:14), he is willing to forgive us for our failures. God knows we are weak and that we sometimes do foolish things. He may become disappointed in us, but he never gives up on us. He keeps giving us a second chance."

Next, show everyone the ashes. You might say something like, "For many centuries, Christians have used the season of Lent as a time to think about God's love for us. They use ashes like this to remind everyone that we are of the dust of the earth and need God's second chance."

Rub your finger in the ashes and make the sign of a cross on the forehead of a family member. Explain, "During the season of Lent, some ministers have their members in the church come forward and have a cross of ash put on their forehead. As the minister makes the cross he says to them, 'Remember, you are dust.'"

Mark the rest of the family. Allow for giggles from little ones. New ideas often cause anxiety. Ask everyone how they feel about being called dust. Allow for response.

PRAYER   Join hands and pray, thanking God for remembering what we really are and asking him to always help us in our weakness.

ASSIGNMENT

Ask each family member to make a list or draw a picture of some of the ways humans are part of creation. They may also make a list or illustrate how we are different. Encourage them to bring their work to the family worship tomorrow night.

 ### Second Day (Thursday)

Light One Purple Candle

Sin in the World

SCRIPTURE READING	Romans 5:12-19
MATERIALS NEEDED	Three pieces of paper or poster board large enough for everyone to see. (Letter size is large enough.) On the first poster write the word *SIN*. On the second write the word *BLAME*. On the third write the word *JESUS*.
LESSON	Enlist one family member to light the candle. You may want to have the same person do the same job for a week at a time. Call on another family member prepared to read the Scripture passage. (This reading is a little tough. You may need an adult or older teen to tackle it.)
DISCUSSION	After the reading, hold up the poster with the word *SIN* printed on it. Invite everyone to offer his or her own definition. After everyone has struggled with it for a few minutes say something like, "Sin is doing something we know God does not approve of." Continue by saying

something like, "When I do something wrong, who can I blame?"

Hold up the poster with the word *BLAME* written on it. Parents, help children out by having a couple of examples ready. For instance, "Well I lost my temper at work and said something to a coworker I should not have. But she made me do it; she made me angry. It was her fault I did the wrong thing!" Allow children to imagine some examples of blame after they get the idea.

When everyone has finished ask, "But is it really true that someone can force us to do the wrong thing? Who can we really blame?" (Only ourselves!)

Explain that the passage read tonight almost sounds as if it is blaming Adam for our sin. But that is not what it really means. Adam was the first to sin, and sin is in the world because Adam sinned first. But we choose to sin all on our own. We don't sin because of Adam, we sin because of us. We sin in the same way Adam did. Ask, "How do you think God feels about our sin?" (Angry, disappointed, hurt—these are all possible responses.) "What do you think God wants to do about our sin?" (Punish us, help us, and so forth.)

Hold up the poster with the word *JESUS* written on it. You might explain this poster by saying, "This is how God feels about the sin in our world. God is so determined to free us from sin's power and influence that he sent Jesus into the world to redeem us and help us.

"It is true that sin is in the world because of the failure of one man, Adam. We all share in that failure when we do things we know are wrong. However, there is also hope and help in the world because of the success of one man. That man was Jesus. His faithfulness has made it possible for us to do the right thing—to please God and love him."

PRAYER

Join hands and pray, thanking God for freeing us from sin's power and influence. Thank him for sending the man Jesus to help us escape Adam's fate.

ASSIGNMENT

Ask family members to share their lists or show their pictures from yesterday. Allow everyone an opportunity to share an example of different ways we participate in creation. Afterwards say something like, "Tomorrow, make a list or draw a picture of the ways we sin." (Be sure to promise "amnesty" for any first-time confessions that may result from this assignment.)

 **Third Day (Friday)**

Light One Purple Candle

More Alive than Dead

SCRIPTURE READING	Ephesians 2:1-10
MATERIALS NEEDED	Two posters made into the shape of gravestones. If possible, use gray poster paper with black letters for the first poster. Write on it: "Here Lies Adam. Dead of Sin." If possible prepare the other poster on white paper with the lettering in a bright color. On this poster write: "Here Stand the Children of God. Alive in Christ!"
LESSON	Light the candle and call on a designated member to read the Scripture selection. After the reading hold up the gravestone poster. Say, "Sin caused Adam to die. He did not drop dead and quit breathing. He died in another way. Inside his heart and mind he died because he was no longer able to be close to God. Any time a person is unable to be close to God, he is, in some sense, dead. He doesn't know the way he should live, and he ends up following the wrong advice and the wrong teaching."

DISCUSSION

Explain that this is what tonight's Scripture reading is talking about. These words were written to some people who knew they were once dead in their sins and were wandering around lost and confused. That is what our sin does to us.

Say, "But God was not willing to leave us in our sin and our death. He did not want this kind of gravestone over us." (Hold up the gravestone poster again.) "Instead, he wants us to have this kind of sign over us." (Hold up the other poster.) "God wants us alive in Christ, not dead in our sin. That is why Jesus came into the world to break the power of sin and to make us alive in his own life."

Ask, "How does this happen?" The answer is, that is what Easter is all about. Read a part of the Scripture again: "Even when we were dead through our trespasses, [God] made us alive together with Christ . . . and raised us up with him" (vv. 5-6). Explain that when God raised Jesus from the dead on the first Easter Sunday, he released the power of resurrection into the world to overcome the power of sin.

We have all sinned. But we do not have to settle for sin. We can rejoice in the power of resurrection. We can celebrate being alive in Christ and being free from sin's power.

PRAYER

Join hands and thank God for making us alive with his Son. Ask God to help us live in a way pleasing to him. Ask him to help us celebrate the life we share with Jesus.

ASSIGNMENT Allow members to share the lists or pictures of examples of sin. Talk for a minute about how that sin causes a kind of death. Parents may promote understanding by giving their examples first. Encourage family members to find examples of the way God brings life out of death in nature. This is a partial picture of what he has done for us in Christ. You may live in an area in which Spring is well in progress. Budding plants and cocoons are examples of life out of death. Smaller children may need help with this. Bring examples to worship tomorrow.

 **Fourth Day (Saturday)**

Light One Purple Candle

The Hope of Forgiveness

SCRIPTURE
READING

Psalm 130

MATERIALS
NEEDED

Any black object that can be held easily in your hand. This might be a black ball, a black coffee cup, or a black hair brush. If none of these are available, use the SIN poster from the second day. Trim the edges so that only the letters themselves remain.

LESSON

Ask the designated family member to light one candle. Read or have someone read Psalm 130.

DISCUSSION

Begin your worship time together by allowing family members to share the results of yesterday's assignment. What examples of life and death in nature did they find? Allow for questions and discoveries.

    Move from this discussion of life and death in nature to life and death in people. Briefly review some of the topics already discussed this week. Say something like, "The

Bible states clearly that our sin, our disobedience, displeases God. We know that and feel guilty about it. After a while, something dies inside of us (topic of the third day of this week). But God is not willing to leave us in this situation. God has something for us that helps us."

Hold up the object or poster. Continue by saying something like, "Pretend this . . . (the black object) is our sin. God can see it plainly. Seeing it makes him unhappy. God wants us to trust him and turn away from our sin. When we are willing to do this, God forgives us of our sin."

As you say this, move the object or poster behind your back. Continue, "When God forgives us, he removes our sin from his sight. He still sees us, and he still loves us. But he chooses to put our sin away. That is what the word *forgiveness* means—to put away, out of sight.

"That is what Jesus' life, death, and resurrection means for us. In Jesus, God has made a way to put our sin out of the way once for all."

PRAYER

Pass the object or poster around to each family member. Invite them to pray one at a time: "Lord, thank you for putting my sin out of your sight in Jesus." As they pray the prayer, ask each family member to move the object or poster behind his or her back. After everyone has had an opportunity to "hide their sins," conclude by praying the prayer in Psalm 130. Substitute your family name for "Israel" in verse 8.

ASSIGNMENT   Invite family members to think of people who may need our forgiveness. Someone may have made us angry or hurt our feelings—in others words, sinned against us. Think of ways we can put their sins out of our sight. Little ones may need help with this. Their issues may be sharing toys or fighting with siblings.

 **Fifth Day (Sunday)**

Light One Purple Candle

Emptied of Glory

SCRIPTURE READING	Philippians 2:1-11
MATERIALS NEEDED	One large glass or jar filled with water and an empty jar that will hold the same amount of water but with a different shape. The greater the difference in shape between the two glasses or jars, the better this exercise will work.
LESSON	Have someone light the candle. Call on the assigned family member to read the Scripture passage. You may want to point out that many scholars believe that verses 6-11 are part of an ancient hymn early Christians sang in their worship services. After the reading you might begin by asking: "What does it mean to be in the form of God? in the form of a human?"
DISCUSSION	Hold up the glass or jar full of water. Continue by saying, "Notice the water in the jar. The water takes on the form or shape of the jar completely."

Empty the water in the full jar into the empty jar. |

Point out that the water has now taken the form of the second jar or glass. The water is the same, but the form is different. In a way, that is what God has done in Jesus. Our Scripture reading said that Jesus was in the form of God. But he "emptied himself, taking the form of a servant." Jesus poured himself out of his God form and poured himself into a human form—and not just a human, but a servant, a humble working person.

Ask, "Why do you think God did this? Why did he want Jesus to pour himself out of God form and into human form?" Allow everyone to struggle with the question for a few moments.

Jesus emptied himself of all his power and glory and became a human being. As a human, Jesus made contact with us and began to teach us how to be free from the sin that keeps hurting us. He also died for us, and through his death and resurrection, he provides us a way to be alive with him.

Conclude by saying something like, "This is why it is possible to say that Jesus lives in our hearts. Just as he was poured into a human body, God can also pour him into our lives when we let him in."

PRAYER

Join hands and lead in a prayer giving thanks for the way God chose to come into our world. Thank God for coming to us as a human being and for dying for our sin.

ASSIGNMENT   Have everyone in the family think of at least one way
                    they might serve God. "How can we be servants to God?
                    What sort of things might we do?" Draw a picture of your
                    example, or be prepared to discuss this at the next wor-
                    ship time.

 **Sixth Day (Monday)**

Light One Purple Candle

The Word Made Flesh

SCRIPTURE
READING

John 1:1-15

MATERIALS
NEEDED

Try to catch an ant and put it in a jar. A housefly or
a harmless bug, even a worm, will work just as well.
(Goldfish will also work if you have a small fishbowl or
tank you can bring to the table or place where you are
worshiping.

LESSON

Light one candle and read the Scripture passage for
this session. Show everyone your example (the ant or
whatever). Say something like, "Wouldn't you love to
be able to talk to the ants? (or goldfish?) Wouldn't it
be exciting to know what they know and to listen to
their stories?

"Imagine there were a colony of ants right in the way of a
huge bulldozer. Most people don't like ants because they are
often a nuisance, but just suppose, for some reason, you
wanted to help the ants, to warn them. But no matter how

loudly you shout, the ants cannot hear you. What would you do?" Allow everyone to try to come up with solutions.

DISCUSSION

After a few moments continue by saying something like, "Imagine you found a way to turn yourself into an ant. You could go right into the anthill and warn all the ants in their own language what was about to happen. You could lead them to a safe place away from any danger." Explain that, in a way, that is what God has done in Jesus. Jesus was with God, was just like God. But Jesus became "flesh." That means he became a human being just like us. Why? Because we were in trouble. Our sin was killing us. God had shouted and shouted through prophets, and Moses, and others. But we couldn't or wouldn't hear. So God sent Jesus to us to talk to us in our own language. He sent Jesus to lead us out of danger and into a safe place. God the Son became human along with us and came to help us in a way we could understand. In Jesus we can see and hear God speaking to us.

PRAYER

Join hands for prayer. Before you pray, have everyone notice the hand they are holding. The skin may be soft, or it may be rough. Our hands are covered with flesh. Jesus one day had hands of flesh much like the hands we are holding. In your prayers, thank Jesus for becoming flesh and coming into our world.

ASSIGNMENT   God is still making himself known through flesh even today. Have family members try to guess how God is still doing that.

 **Seventh Day (Tuesday)**

Light One Purple Candle

Passing the Test

SCRIPTURE
READING

Hebrews 2:14-18; Matthew 4:1-11

MATERIALS
NEEDED

A fairly heavy object. If any family members are weight lifters, a dumbbell would be perfect. You will need something children will have difficulty lifting but an adult can lift easily.

LESSON

Ask a family member to light the candle. Call on the designated person to read the Scripture passages. Read the Hebrews passage first.

DISCUSSION

Begin the discussion by asking, "What does it mean to be tempted?" Allow everyone to respond. Affirm responses. Then say something like, "The Bible says Jesus was tempted in the same way we are. There is even a story in Matthew of how the devil tempted Jesus.

"The word *tempt* in the Bible means more than just trying to lead someone to do something wrong. The word also means 'test.' When the devil met Jesus, he was testing him to see how strong he was—to see how strong his love for God was.

"Now, you might think that because Jesus was the Son of God that he had special strength to win the test." Hold up the weighty object you have secured for this lesson. Invite children to try and lift it. They will struggle. After they have all tried, pick up the weight. Show how easy it is for you. "This weight is not a test for my strength. It is for you, but not for me. That is the way some people think about Jesus' test. They think that because he was the Son of God, he was too strong for the devil.

"But wait a minute! Didn't the Bible say that Jesus was tested just like we are? Yes. That means that when Jesus emptied himself of glory (fifth day of Lent) and became flesh (sixth day of Lent), he also took on the same strength of a real human person.

"So, how did Jesus win the test against the devil? How did Jesus manage to say no to the offers the devil made?" The answer is, Jesus won the test the same way we must win. When we want to do God's will more than anything else, we will be strong to win the tests we must face. Remember, one of the reasons Jesus became a real human person was to show us how real human persons are supposed to live.

As you close this first week, invite family members to recall one thing they have learned this week.

PRAYER   Lead in prayer, thanking God for sending Jesus to us and helping us to be real persons.

ASSIGNMENT   Think of at least one way you have been tested in the last month. Bring an example to the worship time tomorrow. (School tests count!)

The Promise to Abraham

INTRODUCTION TO
the Second Week of Lent

God was not willing to leave us trapped in the deathly effects of our sin. We know now that his ultimate solution was to send Jesus to rescue us and lead us to life. But Jesus only appeared at the end of a long, carefully prepared process. God took many special steps to prepare the human race for the arrival of his Son. The beginning of that careful process was God's call to Abraham.

With Abraham, God began to unfold his intention. God initiated a covenant with Abraham. A covenant is a special kind of agreement. He promised

Abraham "blessings." He also promised Abraham that his children would help the whole world experience blessing.

These promises to Abraham make up an important part of God's plan for all people. Through Abraham, God called Israel, David, and the Suffering Servant who was none other than Jesus the Christ. In Christ, God continues to call out a new people. And it is the new people of God, the followers of Jesus Christ, who are now the heirs of the promises made to Abraham.

As you begin this week, take a moment and help your children understand the key words connected with Abraham. Those words are *promise, blessing, covenant,* and *heir.* If you own something that was left to you by a deceased relative, that would make an excellent object lesson.

For the next seven days we are going to study different aspects of Abraham's calling. As we do, we are seeking to understand what God is calling us to do. What promises does God make to us through this great man of faith? What covenant does God make with us? How are we heirs of the promise? Answers to these questions are found in the Easter miracle.

 **First Day (Wednesday)**

Light Two Purple Candles

Abraham and Sarah's Invitation

SCRIPTURE READING	Genesis 12:1-4
MATERIALS NEEDED	Try to locate a printed invitation. If no one has had a wedding or birthday party recently, simply take a piece of paper and write in large colorful letters, "You Are Invited!"
LESSON	Call on the designated family member to light two purple candles. Explain that we are now beginning our second week of Lent. Remind everyone that the word *lent* means preparation. We are preparing for the resurrection of Jesus. Read the Scripture passage. Hold up the printed invitation you have, or the one you have made.
DISCUSSION	Ask everyone, "How does it make you feel when you get a special invitation from someone?" Allow everyone to respond. Encourage family members to recall specific invitations they have received. Continue by saying, "Receiving an invitation from someone makes us feel

special. An invitation makes us feel important. God gave Abraham a special invitation. Abraham was invited by God to help him start an important event—the coming of Jesus as the Christ.

"This was a hard invitation for Abraham to answer. He had to leave his home and travel to a land he had never seen before. He also had to believe that God would help him and his wife Sarah have a child—even though they were very old!

"Abraham said yes to God's invitation. That is why we think of Abraham as 'Father Abraham.' God kept his promises to Abraham and Sarah. He gave them a son. He also kept another promise to Abraham. Through the descendants of Abraham the whole world has been blessed. Why?" Because the descendants of Abraham include Jesus.

PRAYER

Join hands and give thanks to God for keeping his promises. Thank him also for giving an invitation to Abraham. Abraham is part of God's plan to help us find life. He is part of the plan on the way to the fulfillment of Easter.

ASSIGNMENT

Encourage family members to make a list of friends or family members that they might invite to the worship service at your church this coming Sunday.

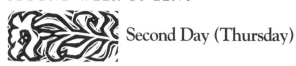 **Second Day (Thursday)**

Light Two Purple Candles

Going with God

SCRIPTURE READING	Hebrews 11:8-10
MATERIALS NEEDED	Play an imaginary game. Call the game "Would you go with me if . . ." Everyone should have a chance to come up with an interesting journey. Here are some suggestions to get started. "Would you go with me if I were traveling to Alaska without any shoes?" "Would you climb a mountain with me if we were both blindfolded?" "Would you travel to Africa with me if we only had one peanut butter sandwich for a whole month?" Have some fun with this. Adults and older siblings should go first so that younger children will have time to make up their own journey.
LESSON	After everyone has taken a turn (or two) light the candles and read the Scripture. Say something like "Abraham and Sarah were asked by God 'Would you go with me if . . . ?' Would they leave home and travel to a land they had never

seen? Would they go with God believing they would have a son even though they were both very old? Would they trust the promises of God enough to follow him in the adventure of their lives?"

The answer to all these questions is yes! Abraham and Sarah had faith in God. They were willing to trust God and go with him where he was leading.

DISCUSSION

Tell the group, "That is what God wants from all of us. He wants us to trust him. He wants us to follow him. He wants us to do what he says. If we will, then he can bless us and help us.

"Abraham and Sarah were not sure how their lives would turn out. We are not sure either. Life is like the game we played—Would you go if . . . ? Would we grow up if we knew it was going to be hard? Would we have children if we knew they would get sick?

"In other words, living life is a matter of faith. We simply don't know how things will turn out. We are all just like Abraham and Sarah. We are on a journey, but we are not sure where we will end up. We just know we are following God to Easter."

PRAYER

Close your worship time in prayer, asking God to be your guide. Ask the Lord to help all of us be faithful followers.

ASSIGNMENT

Ask family members to draw a map of their lives: Where you have come from, where you are going. If you have moved, include actual locations. If you have always lived in the same house, the map will be about growing rather than moving. Your map will feature baby beds, tricycles, dolls, and school desks. Little ones may need some help with the maps. This is a good way to see what your children are planning for the future.

 **Third Day (Friday)**

Light Two Purple Candles

The Children of Faith

SCRIPTURE
READING

Galatians 3:6-9

MATERIALS
NEEDED

Bring a copy of everyone's birth certificate. If these certificates are not available for some reason, bring crayons and
paper and allow everyone to make a birth certificate. Be
sure to include date of birth and names of parents.

LESSON

Call on a designated family member to light two candles.
Call on another to read the Scripture passage. After the
reading, call attention to the birth certificates (make
them at this time if necessary). Say something like,
"These certificates provide important information. They
show when and where we were born. They show our
blood type and who our doctor was. But they also show
who our parents were."

DISCUSSION

Now hold up the Bible. Continue by saying, "According to our Scripture reading for today, if we have faith

in Christ, we are children of Abraham (v. 7). That means that because we trust Jesus, every promise that was made to Abraham is true for us as well. All the blessings that God promised Abraham are also promised to us.

"If we had a birth certificate from God, it would say that we are the children of faith. In other words, because Abraham and Sarah believed in God—that is, they had faith, and because we also believe in God, we are now the children of God.

"But what does that mean? What does it mean to say that we are 'children of faith' or 'children of God'? It means that God has invited us to be part of his family. He has worked through Abraham and Sarah and Jesus to create a special people called 'The People of God.' When we trust Jesus, we become part of that family.

"What do you think God wants his people to do? (Allow time for response.) God wants his people to do exactly what he asked Abraham and Sarah to do. He wants us to obey him. He wants us to trust him. And he wants us to be a blessing to others."

PRAYER

Close your worship time in prayer. Thank God for loving us and being a loving Father to all of us. Thank him for allowing us to be part of his family. Ask the Lord to help us be a blessing to others.

ASSIGNMENT   Encourage everyone to come up with at least one way we can be a blessing to someone else. When you think of a way, go do it. Plan to give a short report tomorrow of what you came up with.

 **Fourth Day (Saturday)**

Light Two Purple Candles

Earning a Place in the Family?

SCRIPTURE READING	Romans 4:1-12
MATERIALS NEEDED	Bring a recent pay stub or whatever your employer gives you to indicate your earnings. A W-2 form will work, or even a tax return. What you are looking for is something to illustrate "earnings."
LESSON	Call on the designated family member to light two candles. The Scripture reading should probably be done by an adult or older sibling. The passage will be clear enough by the end of this study, but some of the concepts are difficult for a child to grasp (and pronounce).
DISCUSSION	After the Scripture reading, pass around the pay stub or tax form. Explain to everyone that this is proof your employer provides of how much you have earned. When you work a certain number of hours, or accomplish a certain amount of work, you earn a certain amount of money.

Then say something like, "This is how we earn money. But how do we earn other things? For example, how do you earn your food in our house? Or how do you earn your bed? How do you earn the right to be called 'son' or 'daughter'?"

Allow children a moment to struggle with these questions. Some may mention chores or other household responsibilities. Be sure to say no to every suggestion that children must earn their place in the family.

As everyone begins to run out of ideas, say something like, "We can earn wages for our work, but you cannot earn a place in a family. Your place in the family is yours simply because of who you are. You are our children, and for that reason you are part of the family.

"That is what Paul was trying to say about Abraham and Sarah. Their faith did not earn them a place in God's family. Their faith helped them see that God cared for them and loved them. They did not earn their place through hard work or even courage. They were given their place in God's family because God loved them and cared for them.

"All of us are children of God through faith. But our faith does not buy our place with God. We do not earn his love. Our faith helps us see what is already true. We are able to see that God loves us and wants us safe. He also wants us to be part of the family. Why? Because we were born and are alive."

PRAYER

Join hands and thank God for your family. Then thank God for his family. Thank him for including in his family all those who believe in him. Ask the Lord to help you help others discover the truth about his love. Remember, we do not earn God's love; we find it through faith.

ASSIGNMENT

Ask family members to report on yesterday's assignment. How did they decide to be a blessing to someone else? Allow a moment for everyone to respond. Say, "We understand now that even though God wants us to do things for him, that does not mean we have to earn his love." Encourage everyone to follow through on their decision to be a blessing in someone's life.

 **Fifth Day (Sunday)**

Light Two Purple Candles

Someone Greater than Abraham

SCRIPTURE READING	John 8:51-58
MATERIALS NEEDED	Paper and markers or crayons
LESSON	Light two candles. Call on the designated family member to read the Scripture passage. Distribute the paper and markers or crayons. Instruct everyone to draw a picture of someone they think is a great person. This might be a political figure, a cartoon character, or even a parent or grandparent. Allow time for the pictures to be well in progress.
DISCUSSION	Take a few moments for each person to show his or her work and explain why their character is great. Be sure to affirm everyone's effort.

Continue by saying, "We have learned this week that Abraham was certainly a great person. He and Sarah believed God's promises and followed where God led them. Because of these decisions, Abraham was considered the father of the Jewish people. They called Abraham a 'patriarch.' That means Abraham was a 'founding father.'

"In our Scripture reading for today, some of the Jewish people were upset by Jesus' teaching about the resurrection. They said, 'Abraham, our great hero, died a long time ago. Are you claiming to be greater than Abraham?' Jesus' answer really surprised his opponents. 'The great Abraham,' he began, 'longed to see the day I would arrive. In fact, he did see it, and rejoiced' (v. 56)!

"In other words, Abraham's purpose in life was to see the fulfillment of the promise. He wanted to see the Messiah. And because he was faithful, he was alive with God. When Jesus left heaven to come to earth to save us, Abraham saw it and was glad.

"But don't miss the point! As great and important as Abraham was, to us and to God, he was not as great as Jesus. Abraham was one step on the way, but Jesus was the fulfillment of all the promises made by God to Abraham.

"We are moving steadily toward Easter. As we go, we are discovering how carefully God prepared the world for the coming of his Son. Every major figure in the Bible was just like Abraham. They were waiting for Jesus to appear. They were waiting for the promises."

PRAYER   Close your worship time with prayer, thanking God for his faithfulness to us. Thank him for the great faith of Abraham and Sarah. But thank him especially for the great gift of his Son, Jesus the Christ. After all, he is the one who made all the promises possible in the first place.

ASSIGNMENT   Invite family members to think again about their definitions of greatness. Point out that sometimes it is not the strong or powerful who are great, but humble servants. Encourage family members to think of someone who is a genuine servant in your community. Write that person a thank-you note.

 **Sixth Day (Monday)**

Light Two Purple Candles

The Comforter of the Poor

SCRIPTURE READING	Luke 16:19-25
MATERIALS NEEDED	A plate with a few crumbs of bread on it
LESSON	Ask a family member to light two candles. Call on the designated family member to read the Scripture passage for the day.
DISCUSSION	Begin by saying, "God invited Abraham to a difficult task. Abraham had to leave home, he had to leave his parents, he had to leave his relatives. He and Sarah traveled to a place they had never seen before. They did all of this so that God might be able to fulfill his dream of calling out a people dedicated to helping the world worship and praise the one true God.
	"Don't you imagine that Abraham and Sarah spent some lonely nights wondering if they had done the right

thing? Of course we know they really did the right thing. We also know that God blessed them both richly for their faith.

"Years later, during the time of Jesus, when the descendants of Abraham were literally more numerous than the sands of the sea, two of those descendants were found in a strange relationship. One was Lazarus a poor beggar. The other was a rich man. Both of those people were children of Abraham by birth. One was rich; one was poor. The poor man was hoping that the great riches of his rich brother would help him out of his poverty. He was willing to settle for the crumbs that fell from the rich man's table."

Hold up the plate of bread crumbs. Continue by saying, "Not much of a lunch is it? Apparently the rich man was so unfeeling that he would not even give Lazarus his throwaway food. His unwillingness to help his brother was an indication that the rich man did not love God. If we love God, we also love our neighbor.

"After a while the rich man died and went to hades, the place of the dead. Lazarus also died and was carried into the bosom of Abraham. There he was comforted by the great father of his faith.

"The rich man also wanted to be comforted, but Abraham told him, 'You had your chance to be faithful, but you chose not to be.' Then Abraham said something truly strange. He said that even with Moses and the prophets, and even with someone coming back from the dead, if people want to be selfish, they will. In other words, just because we have Bibles and read them to people, and just because we believe in Easter and preach it hopefully, and just because we live good moral lives, does not mean that people are going to believe us.

"What is missing? What else could we do? Maybe what is missing is what was missing from the life of the rich man. Maybe the most important step we can take is to love our neighbors enough to help them with their pain and need. Perhaps in that act of faith we will find a way to really be like Abraham."

PRAYER

Join hands and pray for the needy persons in our world. Ask God to help us know how we might help them. Pray also that we would not turn our back on the hurting and the hungry.

ASSIGNMENT

Decide together as a family one way you all might be able to help a needy family. You might give food and clothes to a relief shelter. You might donate money to a local soup kitchen. You may want to volunteer to serve meals one Saturday at that same soup kitchen. There may be a poor family in your community you could befriend. The needs around us are always greater than the resources needed to meet them. Choose one. Have family members take note of how they feel while they are doing their work. How did they make others feel with their efforts?

 **Seventh Day (Tuesday)**

Light Two Purple Candles

"You Are the Fulfillment of the Promise"

SCRIPTURE READING

Acts 3:17-25

MATERIALS NEEDED

If you have recently paid off an installment loan with a coupon book, try to locate the empty book. Maybe you have a contract that has been completed. A bill of sale will work. If none of these are available, simply take a sheet of paper and write across the front of it, "Paid in Full." We are looking for a way to illustrate the successful completion of an agreement.

LESSON

Light two candles. Call on the family member responsible to read the Scripture for today. After the reading, show everyone the "paid in full" item you brought with you. Say something like, "This coupon book represents a long effort on our part. We had to work hard to pay this off. Now the car (or television, or whatever) is the fulfillment of our agreement. We own it now, free and clear."

DISCUSSION

Continue by saying, "The long, hard agreement between God and Abraham is also paid in full. The fulfillment of that promise was the coming of Jesus as the Messiah. But there is one more part to the agreement that we have not talked about yet."

Read Acts 3:25 and say something like, "You are the children of Abraham. You are the fulfillment of the promise. God was looking ahead to Jesus, that is true. But the purpose of Jesus' coming was to create new people, new children, who would love him, serve him, and obey him in the same way Abraham did.

"Promises made to the people of Israel are now made to everyone. Promises made to God's chosen people now apply to his new chosen people. With the coming of Jesus, every person in the world has the opportunity to become part of God's family. That is what the writer of Acts means when he says, 'And in your posterity shall all the families of the earth be blessed' (v. 25).

"Abraham was the beginning of an important plan. He was faithful and God blessed him. Through him, the whole world has been blessed. But there were other faithful persons involved. Next week we will look at the promises made to Israel. We will see how God carefully moved through history to bring about the fulfillment of his promise in us."

PRAYER   Close your worship time in prayer, thanking God for all
                    the faithful people who serve him. Ask that he will help us
                    to serve faithfully as well.

ASSIGNMENT   Encourage everyone to draw a picture or write a short para-
                    graph describing one way God worked through Abraham
                    to help bring Jesus into the world.

The Promise to Israel

INTRODUCTION TO
the Third Week of Lent

The promises God made to Abraham were passed on to the people of Israel. God chose Moses to be his spokesperson. Through Moses, God made it possible for the people of Israel to escape the bondage of Egypt. As the people of Israel followed Moses into the wilderness, they began a journey toward God. That journey would take them by a holy mountain and eventually into the Promised Land.

The covenant we have come to call the Ten Commandments was the fruit of that invitation. In the covenant with Israel God was continuing the covenant he made with Abraham. He was seeking through the people of Israel a way to bless the entire world.

Often, the people of Israel thought that because they were God's chosen people, they occupied a privileged place among the people of the world. They thought that because they were God's special treasure, they could do no wrong. They did not understand that extraordinary privilege calls for extraordinary obedience.

The people of Israel also misunderstood the purpose of the covenant. They began to call it "law" and sought to enforce it. They did not understand that the commandments of God were instructions designed to explain life and to show the principles of right and wrong. The law, because it could only show what right and wrong were, proved how guilty mankind was, and that guilt brought death instead of life. But the law was good, because it showed mankind how much they needed a savior from sin. God from the very beginning had a plan by which he was going to save his people and bless the world through them. The law only showed how bad they were—it could not make people better.

For that to be possible, God would make a new covenant. The terms of the new covenant would be the life, death, and resurrection of Jesus of Nazareth.

 **First Day (Wednesday)**

Light Three Purple Candles

God Calls Israel to Be His People

SCRIPTURE
READING

Exodus 19:5-6; 20:1-17

MATERIALS
NEEDED

Any kind of contract. If you financed your car or have a home mortgage, then you have a contract that sets forth the terms of repayment. If you have no contracts in your house, take paper and pencil and make one. Be sure to include two parts. The first part is what you promise to give. The second part is what you expect to receive.

LESSON

Call on the designated family member to light three purple candles. Point out that we are now in the third week of Lent. *Lent* means preparation. Call on a family member to read the two passages from Exodus.

After the Scripture reading you may want to review briefly the events leading up to the giving of the covenant at Mount Sinai. The introduction to this week will provide some information. You may also scan Exodus chapters 1–19 in preparation.

DISCUSSION

Show everyone the contract you have brought or made. You might say something like, "Contracts are very useful tools. They help people to be able to have things they might not be able to get in any other way. A house, for instance, is very expensive. But a bank or mortgage company will loan a family the money they need to buy a house. But the family must promise to pay all of the money back eventually. The bank and the family sign a contract. The bank promises to loan the money. The family promises to pay it back. The bank makes a profit on the interest. The family gets to buy their own home.

"God offered the people of Israel a kind of contract. He called it a covenant. In this covenant God promised to be God to the people of Israel. He promised to help them and take care of them. In return, the people of Israel promised to behave in special ways." (Read the Ten Commandments, Exod. 20:1-17.)

"God wanted his people to be special. He wanted the world to be able to tell the difference between his people and everybody else. He wanted his people to help other people learn of him and know him. That was Israel's part of the covenant."

Ask everyone to answer this question: "How can the Ten Commandments help us teach people about God?" Allow time for everyone to respond. The answer is: God wants us to know that he is holy and that he wants us to be holy.

PRAYER   Close your worship time in prayer, thanking God for keeping his promises. Ask him to help us keep our end of the bargain.

ASSIGNMENT   Have family members try to write the Ten Commandments from memory. Have them bring their efforts to worship tomorrow. Ask them to decide which one of the commandments is the most difficult to follow.

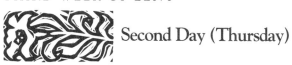 **Second Day (Thursday)**

Light Three Purple Candles

The Purpose of the Covenant (Law)

SCRIPTURE
READING

Galatians 3:15-26

MATERIALS
NEEDED

A rule book. You may use one from a favorite sport such as softball or basketball. The rules printed under the lid of your favorite board game will also work. Call on a family member to light the candles and read the Scripture reading. After the reading, show everyone the rule book.

LESSON

Ask, "What is the purpose of having rules in a game?" Most will say to make sure no one cheats, or that everyone plays fairly. Affirm these as part of the true purpose of rules. However, there is another purpose for a rule book. The rules help people who have never played the game learn how to play.

DISCUSSION

"In our Scripture reading for today, Paul discusses whether or not the covenant made with Israel did away with the covenant made to Abraham. Paul says that it did not. The covenant to Israel was given to be our "custodian" (v. 24) until Jesus came to establish the new covenant.

"In other words, the purpose of the old covenant with Israel was to help us know the rules and play the game (of life) until God was ready to reveal his Son to us. God knew that we could not keep them perfectly, and realizing we couldn't would make us see the need for the Savior whom God sent. Later we will see that Jesus did not do away with the covenant made with Israel. Instead he fulfilled it (Matt. 5:17-20).

"For now let us understand that the purpose of the covenant with Israel was to help us know how God wants us to live. Not just what the rules are, although that is very important. But also how life works."

Take a moment and see how everyone did in writing the Ten Commandments from memory. Fill out the list so everyone has all ten in front of them. Ask, "Which of the Ten Commandments teach us how life is supposed to work. Give an example."

Allow everyone an opportunity to think about this. Provide help to children as needed.

PRAYER

Close your worship time with prayer. Thank God for taking steps to help us live full, meaningful lives. Thank him for calling the people of Israel to carry the promise of the covenant.

ASSIGNMENT   Find out which commandment each family member found most difficult to obey. Encourage family members to come up with at least one idea how they might better observe this particular life instruction. Be prepared to report tomorrow.

 **Third Day (Friday)**

Light Three Purple Candles

What the Old Covenant Could Not Do

SCRIPTURE READING	Romans 7:7-12; 8:2-4.
MATERIALS NEEDED	Use the same rule book from yesterday.
LESSON	Call on a designated family member to read the Scripture selection. You may want to ask an older sibling or handle this reading yourself. After the reading hold up the rule book again. Say something like, "You know, if it were not for this rule book, there would not be any cheaters. Think about the rule in basketball that says it is cheating to grab a shooter's arm while he is shooting. Or think about the rule in checkers that says you can move only one piece at a time. If we took those rules out of the book, there would never be any cheaters. Right? But what would happen without rules?" (There would be no cheaters, but there also would be no game. The game would not make any sense.)

DISCUSSION

"In a way, that is what Paul is talking about in our Scripture reading for today. The Law didn't enable the people to keep the rules (play the game of life). Instead, according to Paul, what the Law did was make everybody feel guilty about their inability to keep God's commandments, which were to show them their need for a Savior from sin.

"Did the Law fail then? If we expected the Law to make us acceptable to God, then it fails us. For the same reason, rules don't keep people from trying to cheat. Even though the rule in basketball is clear, players still grab the shooter's arm. Right? The Law does not change people on the inside. The Law does not change the minds or the hearts of people. And until we change on the inside, until something happens inside us to make it possible for us to keep God's rules, we will keep falling into the trap of cheating.

"Paul says that in Jesus Christ we finally have a way to keep the Law of God from the inside out. That is the only way it will work. In the life, death, and resurrection of Jesus we are freed from sin and given strength to fulfill the rules of life established by God."

Ask everyone to share the idea they came up with for tackling their one hard commandment. Point out that the first step toward obeying God's rules is having Christ in our hearts. As we follow Christ in love and faith, he helps us do what God has called us to do.

PRAYER   Close your worship in prayer, asking Christ to give us power to live the way he wants us to live. Thank God for sending Jesus as our helper and friend.

ASSIGNMENT   Have everyone try again to write the Ten Commandments from memory. Bring results to worship tomorrow.

 **Fourth Day (Saturday)**

Light Three Purple Candles

The Promise of a New Covenant

SCRIPTURE
READING

Jeremiah 31:27-34

MATERIALS
NEEDED

A piece of paper with the words "Old Covenant" written on it. If you want to be creative, use gray construction paper. Cut the paper in the shape of tablets of stone. Have someone light the candles and read the assigned Scripture text.

LESSON

After the reading, say something like, "The prophet Jeremiah spoke the words in our reading tonight to the people of Israel during one of their darkest moments. The city of Jerusalem was destroyed. The temple was in ruins. The armies of Babylon had taken the city apart and kidnapped thousands of people. These people would be slaves in Babylon.

"The people of Israel could not understand how something like this could happen. They thought that, because they were God's people, God would protect them. They thought that as God's chosen people they could do no wrong. This, of course, was a serious mistake on their part.

"Jeremiah, and other prophets as well, warned the people of Israel that God expected them to live up to the terms of the covenant. If they did not, God would punish them. When they continued to disobey, God allowed the Babylonians to sack the city. The people of Israel would face a lonely exile of seventy years.

"God spoke through Jeremiah to give his hurting people hope." Hold up the paper with the words "Old Covenant" written on it. Crumple it up and throw it aside.

DISCUSSION

Say something like, "The Old Covenant was written on stone. It told the people about right and wrong, but it was unable to help them do what was right. Because they were unable and unwilling to keep God's teaching, they suffered because of it. But God was determined to have a covenant people. He promised through Jeremiah that a new covenant would be given. This time he would write the covenant on the hearts of his people. A covenant written on the heart is written from the inside out (remember yesterday's lesson). A covenant written on the heart not only shows right from wrong but enables us to do the things that please God."

PRAYER

Close your worship time with prayer, thanking God for writing the New Covenant on our hearts in Jesus Christ. Thank him for not giving up on us no matter how much we disappoint him.

ASSIGNMENT

Ask, "How many were able to memorize the Ten Commandments?" One way we know the covenant is in our heart is when it is a part of us. Have everyone think of at least one way the commandments of God are part of our lives simply by the way we act or do things or treat people.

 **Fifth Day (Sunday)**

Light Three Purple Candles

The Hope of a Lasting Covenant

SCRIPTURE
READING

Hebrews 13:14-20

MATERIALS
NEEDED

A large rock

LESSON

Call on a designated family member to light the three purple candles. Have another read the Scripture assignment for the day.

Hold up the rock. Ask, "Who can tell me how this rock became a rock?" If your children are too young to have had any elementary science, they may simply answer "God made it!" Affirm that as a very good answer. However, what you are looking for is the awareness that rocks are formed by earth forces working over long periods of time. The rock you hold in your hand is probably thousands of years old. It has existed for a long time and probably will exist for a long time to come. But the day may come when it crumbles into sand.

DISCUSSION

Say something like, "In our Scripture reading for the day, the writer of the book of Hebrews expresses hope in an 'eternal covenant.' We saw what happened to the people of Israel with their law. It was written on stone and lasted a long time, like our rock. But like the rock, it was not eternal. There came a time when the purpose of the covenant of law was fulfilled and overshadowed by a covenant of grace. The New Covenant, the work of Jesus Christ, is the covenant Jeremiah promised. He is the covenant written on our hearts. Jesus is also the 'eternal covenant' we read about today.

"An eternal covenant does not wear out or go out of date. An eternal covenant cannot be improved. God has given us the best he has to offer in Jesus. An eternal covenant works. If we enter into the New Covenant with Jesus, we can be sure God will bless us and make us part of his new people.

"There is one more thing about an eternal covenant. There is no other. In other words, an eternal covenant is one of a kind, and the best there is, and there is not another. This is it. There are lots of rocks that have been in the world a long time. But there is only one agreement with God that lasts forever. That is the New Covenant offered in the life, death, and resurrection of Jesus of Nazareth."

PRAYER

As you pray today, thank God for taking such care in providing for our needs. Thank God also for paying such a dear price for our New Covenant. The writer of Hebrews says that the eternal covenant was purchased with the blood of Jesus. That is how much he loves us.

ASSIGNMENT

Ask family members to write or draw what they see as the connection between Abraham and the first covenant, and Israel and the covenant of the Law, and Jesus. What is the one thing God is doing? Little ones may need extra help. (Answer: Establish a covenant people.)

 **Sixth Day (Monday)**

Light Three Purple Candles

The Promise to Abraham and the Promise to Israel

SCRIPTURE
READING

Luke 1:67-79

MATERIALS
NEEDED

A Bible

LESSON

Light three purple candles. Call on the family member designated to read the Scripture selected for today. Instruct the reader in advance to emphasize verses 73 and 74 as the passage is read. These are the focal verses for our worship today.

DISCUSSION

After the reading, take the Bible, close it, and hold it flat in your open hand. You might say something like, "In courts of law in America, before witnesses are allowed to give their testimony about something, they must place their hand on a Bible and pledge an oath. That oath usually sounds like this: 'Do you promise to tell the truth, the whole truth, and nothing but the truth, so help you God?'

The witness will then respond, 'I do.' This promise is binding under law. If they lie, they can be arrested.

"In our reading today we heard that God made an oath. He didn't put his hand on a Bible, but he did swear by his own word that he was about to do something. Does anyone remember what that oath was about?" Give everyone a chance to remember. If no one recalls, open the Bible and read Luke 1:73-74 again.

"The promise has two parts. The first part has to do with God's protection. God has promised to save us from anything or anyone that may try to harm us. This part of the promise demonstrates God's love for us. The Cross of Jesus Christ comes from this part of the promise. The death of Jesus is God's way of freeing us from our greatest enemy—death.

"The second part of the oath deals with what God wants. God wants a people. This is what he has wanted all along. From the very beginning in his call to Abraham, he was in the process of calling out a people that would be his. And what is the purpose he has in mind for his people? That is made clear in verse 74. God wants his people to serve him without fear.

"In other words, God wants to give life to us as a free gift. He wants us to be happy and enjoy his beautiful creation. He wants us to take care of each other, especially the weak and hurting among us.

"He also wants us to worship and adore him. Why?" Because if we worship and adore something else, God can't give us his best, and it will result in our dying in sin. If we worship and adore God, we find life. All of this was in God's mind when he called Abraham. It was in his mind when he called Israel to be his people. And it was certainly in his mind when he sent Jesus to make one final call to all people to be his people. He is still calling through Jesus Christ. Ask, "Have we answered and said yes?"

PRAYER

Close your worship time with prayer, asking God to help us fulfill his dream of being a servant people. Pray for special guidance that we will know exactly where and how God wants us to serve.

ASSIGNMENT

Ask everyone to think of at least one way that they serve God at the present time. If they can't think of a way they are serving now, ask them what they can do to begin serving God. Be prepared to give a brief report at the next worship time.

 **Seventh Day (Tuesday)**

Light Three Purple Candles

Jesus, the Fulfillment of the Promise

SCRIPTURE
READING
: Matthew 5:17-20

MATERIALS
NEEDED
: An Alka Seltzer, or some other form of antacid that reacts when placed in water

LESSON
: Light three purple candles. Call on a designated family member to read the Scripture for the day.

DISCUSSION
: After the reading hold up the Alka Seltzer and the glass of water. You might say, "This Alka Seltzer is one kind of medicine for indigestion. However, it only works if I put it in water. Even though everything I need to relieve my upset stomach is in this tablet, it won't help me until I put it into the water. In other words, the tablet is not fulfilled until it goes through all of the planned steps.

"This is what Jesus was talking about in our reading today. The Law had all that we needed, but it had not gone through all the steps. It was written on stone, not on our hearts. God wants us to keep the Law, Jesus makes that clear. But there is only one way to actually keep the Law of God.

"The only way to keep the Law of God in a way that pleases God is by accepting Jesus as the fulfillment of the Law. In other words, the way God is able to write the Law on our hearts is by allowing Jesus into our lives to take charge."

Drop the Alka Seltzer into the water. Let it fizz for a moment. Continue by saying, "As the Alka Seltzer enters the water it is able to fulfill itself and become what it was intended to become. But notice something else. As the Alka Seltzer enters the water, the water itself changes! It is not just water anymore; it is seltzer water.

"The same thing happens to us when Christ enters our lives. We are not just people anymore. We are God's people. The purpose of God is fulfilled in us through Jesus Christ.

"One more comparison. The seltzer water is now ready to be a medicine. I can drink it now and it will help my upset stomach. In the same way, as we become the people of God, we are ready to be used by God to bring healing to our world. In our world there is fear, there is anger, there is pain, and there is poverty. Our world needs healing. How will it come? Healing will come as God works through his people. We are part of God's plan for offering hope and healing to a troubled world."

Call on volunteers to share their assignment from yesterday. How can we be servant people of God? How are we serving now? Affirm responses and encourage new discoveries.

PRAYER

Close your worship time in prayer, thanking God for offering his Son as healing for our world. Thank God for keeping his promises through his Son. Ask God to help us as we try to be his people in a difficult world.

ASSIGNMENT

Invite family members to think of at least one way God has healed us. It may be recovery from an actual illness, or it may be help with a difficult family problem. Little ones may need help understanding the connection between doctors and God's healing. Help them understand that doctors are also servants of God.

The Promise to David

INTRODUCTION TO
the Fourth Week of Lent

The people of Israel found it difficult to be what God wanted them to be. Having God alone for King, and believing in only one God, made them different from every other people with whom they had contact. They felt inferior to other nations. Their neighbors all worshiped more than one god. These neighboring nations also had powerful rulers to lead them. Eventually the people of Israel gave in to their weakness and began to beg for a king like everyone else.

God did not want them to have an earthly king (read 1 Samuel 8) because he wanted to be their king. God had an ideal plan for them, but he knew that the only way they would realize it was to allow them to get what they wanted and learn the hard way. They soon realized what having an earthly king was really like.

God gave them Saul, whose kingship was a disaster from almost the very beginning. But God had mercy on his people. He found a way to teach them about his ideals for a kingly rule. God sought a man "after his own heart." He brought a man to the people of Israel who was committed to doing God's will, ruling in God's favor, and bringing the people into closer relationship with God. This special king was David.

David was the most famous and popular of all Israelite kings. All the kings that followed him were called "sons of David." He became the standard by which all other kings were compared. David also became the symbol for another king who was to come. As time went on, the people of Israel came to believe that the Messiah would be the fulfillment of David's greatest qualities. The Messiah would be the Son of David in the ultimate sense.

How did the people of Israel come to this conclusion? The Bible records some interesting promises made to David. Many of these promises only make sense in the light of Jesus Christ. However, these promises also teach that through David, God was working to fulfill his dream of calling out a servant people.

This coming week's worship activities will focus on the promises made to David. In these promises, the people of Israel were reminded again and again that God had called them out to be a special, servant people.

 **First Day (Wednesday)**

Light Four Purple Candles

David Becomes King of Israel

SCRIPTURE
READING

2 Samuel 5:1-5

MATERIALS
NEEDED

Paper and colored pencils to draw a picture of a shepherd and sheep. If you have access to encyclopedias or other resources with pictures, you may want to use those.

LESSON

Light four purple candles. Take note of the additional candle, explaining that you have now entered the fourth week of Lent. Call on a designated family member to read the Scripture passage. Take a few moments to either draw the shepherd pictures, or share the ones you found elsewhere.

DISCUSSION

Begin your time together by explaining how God felt about Israel having a king. (You may want to read 1 Samuel 8.) God knew that a king would divert the people away from godly pursuits and into earthly pursuits. God wanted direct rule over Israel, but his people were not satisfied with a heavenly king—they wanted to be like everyone else, to have an earthly king.

God had Saul anointed as king, but he proved to be a very bad ruler. But after Saul, God allowed David to take the throne of Israel. The Bible says that David "was a man after God's own heart." He was a shepherd when God anointed him. And he became a shepherd to the people of Israel.

As a shepherd, and as a godly man, David was deeply concerned to lead the people of Israel toward God even as he built up the nation in size and wealth. David made it possible for worship to be centralized in Jerusalem. He brought the tribes together as one people. With the help of the prophet Nathan, David helped to create an awareness that the people of Israel were God's people.

Ask everyone to describe in their own words the difference between a shepherd king and a warrior king. Little ones may need some help. The main difference is that the shepherd king leads his people in worthwhile pursuits—such as becoming a community of faith.

PRAYER

Close the worship time by joining hands in prayer. Thank God for leading us as a gentle shepherd. Thank him for David who heard God's promises and believed them.

ASSIGNMENT

Ask everyone to use the pictures you have drawn or the pictures you found and make up a story about a shepherd king. It does not have to be a biblical story. Encourage everyone to be sure and tell in their story how the shepherd king helps his people.

 Second Day (Thursday)

Light Four Purple Candles

The Promise of God to David

SCRIPTURE
READING

2 Samuel 7:1-29 (cf. Ps. 89:3-4)

MATERIALS
NEEDED

A diagram of a family tree. If you don't have one, make a small one. Go back as many generations as you are able.

LESSON

Light the four purple candles. If possible, use two different Bibles and two different readers for the two passages assigned for today. Otherwise, call on the designated family member to read both passages. Be sure to save the psalm for last. Allow everyone to share their stories about the shepherd king from the assignment of yesterday. Point out that we are about to see another important part of David's life.

DISCUSSION

Take a few moments and discuss your family tree. Share some interesting stories about your family. Help everyone to understand the connection we share with our relatives.

    After the discussion of your family tree, ask family

members to explain the promise God made to David. Allow everyone a chance to answer. The answer, of course, is that God promised David that his descendants would always sit on the throne in Israel. But more! God also promised David that the King of kings, the ultimate King, the Messiah, would also be a descendant (read 2 Sam. 7:13).

Ask how they think the promise made David feel. (Allow time for response.) Ask, "How would this promise to David work with the other promises we have looked at? How is this promise connected to the promise made to Abraham and the promise made to Israel?"

Explain how God is carefully moving events toward his own conclusion. He wants to call out all people as his own people. He wants all people of the earth blessed. His plan for doing that is to ultimately send Jesus to live and die for us.

But God moves slowly with his plan. Sometimes we are slow to notice what he is doing. David was one key step along the way. With David God began to close in on his main goal—to bring into the world a king to call out his people.

PRAYER

As you close your worship tonight, thank God for including all of us as his people. Thank God for taking such careful steps to include everyone. Thank God for David who was an important part of God's plan.

ASSIGNMENT   As a family, select someone from your extended family, per-
              haps a grandparent or an uncle or aunt. Write them a spe-
              cial note of encouragement. Thank them for their role in
              the family. Be sure to note any special help or guidance
              this person has provided through the years.

 **Third Day (Friday)**

Light Four Purple Candles

David, the Image of the Coming King

SCRIPTURE READING	Jeremiah 23:5-6
MATERIALS NEEDED	Be prepared to share with other family members how you learned something from a parent or grandparent. Suggestions might include fishing, carpentry, ceramics, and so on.
LESSON	Light four purple candles. Call on a family member to read the Scripture for the day. Take a moment to make sure you have finished the letter from yesterday's assignment. If you have already mailed it, simply review what you did.
DISCUSSION	Begin your worship time by telling family members about some special skill or talent you learned from your parents or grandparents. Explain how this skill has helped you or enriched your life. Conclude by saying, "When I do things my parents did, I am acting in their image, by their example, even if I do it better."

Point out that David's relationship with the people of Israel and Jesus' relationship with God's people is much the same. The things David accomplished in a small way, ruling over one tiny country, Jesus will accomplish in a great way, ruling over an entire universe. Because of this we can say that David was the image of the coming Christ.

In the same way, the prophet Jeremiah was looking forward to the time when the perfect king would come and rule wisely and fairly. David created a positive image of kingly rule. The perfect King would rule like David, only better.

Take a moment and ask family members (children especially) to think of some things they are learning from their parents. (Help them, but don't prompt them.) Then ask, "What are some things we learn to do from Jesus?" Answer the question for yourself; then encourage everyone to think of an example.

Conclude by saying, "As we do the things Jesus has taught us, we are also part of his image in the world."

PRAYER

Join in prayer, asking God to help us learn how we may give a positive image of him in our world and to help us to learn the lessons he is teaching us. Thank him for loving us and taking time to guide us.

ASSIGNMENT   Ask everyone to make a list of some things they would like to learn from parents. Also make a list of some things everyone would like to learn from God.

 **Fourth Day (Saturday)**

Light Four Purple Candles

The Character of the Coming King

SCRIPTURE
READING

Ezekiel 34:2-24

MATERIALS
NEEDED

Items from a first-aid kit

LESSON

Light four purple candles. The Scripture for tonight is fairly long, but the reading is not difficult. You may want to assign the reading earlier in the day so the designated family member will have a chance to look it over. Read the entire section after lighting the candles.

DISCUSSION

Allow family members a moment to share their work from the assignment from yesterday. Ask them to name some things we would like to learn from our parents and from God. Tell them that tonight we will learn something special about God and his Son.

Show everyone the items from a first-aid kit you have brought with you. You might begin by saying, "Imagine you are out playing. Suddenly you fall down and are injured—scratches and cuts. You run to me because you know I have the first-aid kit. But when you get to me, I refuse to let you have anything out of it. I won't give you any bandages, or Band-Aids, or antibiotic ointment. Nothing. I keep it all for myself. How would that make you feel?" Allow time for response.

Explain how the prophet Ezekiel was dealing with a similar problem. The shepherds he is talking about are leaders of Israel. After the time of David many of them were terrible disappointments. They misused their power, and they took advantage of the people, especially the poor.

The people were hurting. They cried out to their "shepherds" for help, but their cries were ignored. The prophet was assuring them that the coming Messiah, the Son of David, would have a completely different character. He would not treat them in this way.

Apply this truth by explaining how everyone hurts from time to time. We may even hurt so badly that we are tempted to believe no one cares. If that happens, let us remember the Cross and the resurrection of Jesus, the Good Shepherd. The Cross reminds us that Jesus knows our suffering and pain. The Resurrection reminds us that God has the power to bring good even out of death and darkness.

PRAYER

Join hands and thank God for sending us the Good Shepherd. Thank him for caring about our needs and our hurts. Thank him also for providing the things we need to live and to live fully.

ASSIGNMENT

Think of some people you know who may be hurting. These may be people who are sick. They may be people who have lost loved ones. They may be people who have suffered some sort of material loss. Think of a way as a family to offer these people encouragement and hope. You may want to send a card, or maybe bake some cookies. As you do this, keep in mind how God cares about us when we hurt.

 **Fifth Day (Sunday)**

Light Four Purple Candles

The New King Greater than David

SCRIPTURE
READING

Matthew 22:41-46

MATERIALS
NEEDED

Paper and pencil. You are going to ask family members to draw a picture of the "greatest person alive today."

LESSON

Call on a family member to light the candles and read the Scripture for the day.

    As you begin your time of worship, you might say, "Tonight we are going to find out who we all think is the greatest person alive today." Distribute paper and pencils to everyone. If your children are older, allow them to simply write the name of the person they believe is the greatest person alive today. Younger children are encouraged to draw a picture of their person. (Omit Jesus as a candidate. Of course, he is the greatest of all, and he is alive through the Holy Spirit. Nevertheless, we are looking for flesh and blood persons living today to use as an illustration. These people may be astronauts, presidents, or even parents. Try not to blush if your children pick you!)

DISCUSSION

After family members have made their selection, allow them a moment to explain why they believe their "greatest person" is great. Be sure to affirm responses.

Continue by saying something like, "If we had asked this question of the people of Israel, they are likely to have said David. David was the greatest king Israel ever had."

Explain how Jesus, however, went out of his way to help the people of Israel understand that the Messiah, the Son of David, would be even greater than David. In fact, the psalm Jesus quotes (Ps. 110) has David calling the Messiah "Lord"!

Ask, "Why is this important?" It is important because Jesus was not in the world to continue the work of David. David was just the king of Israel. Jesus is King of the universe. The people of Israel needed to understand that even though the Messiah would be like David in his compassion and wisdom, he would also be different from David. As Messiah, Jesus knew he would do some things differently from David, better than David.

God made many promises to David, and David did many wonderful things. This made him a great man in the memory of the people of Israel. However, Jesus was greater than David. His work has touched the whole world. His sacrifice and resurrection has made it possible for all people to call God Father. David could never do that. He was just one step on the way to Easter.

PRAYER

Close with prayer.

ASSIGNMENT

Ask everyone to compare the person they identified as great with Jesus. How do they compare? Where are they similar (fairness, love, forgiveness, etc.)? Where are they different? Encourage family members to name as many differences as possible.

 Sixth Day (Monday)

Light Four Purple Candles

Jesus Proclaimed as the New King

SCRIPTURE READING	Acts 2:29-36
MATERIALS NEEDED	A large piece of poster board or paper. You are going to design a billboard announcing to the world that Jesus is King of kings and Lord of lords.
LESSON	Light the four purple candles. Call on a family member to read the Scripture for today. After the Scripture reading you might begin by saying, "Have you ever noticed the big signs that stand along the highway? These are called billboards. They are used for advertising. What are some of the things you remember seeing advertised on these billboards?" Allow time for everyone to respond.
DISCUSSION	Continue by saying, "Sometimes even churches use billboards to advertise." Hold up the billboard you have made. "When churches advertise, they are seeking ways to tell people that Jesus is King of kings and Lord of lords."

Explain how the church in the book of Acts did not erect any billboards. They did, however, spread the Word of God. Everywhere the early Christians went they found a way to announce that the new King had arrived. (Read Acts 2:36 again.)

This must have been important news for them. A new period in history was beginning. In Jesus, God was making a new start. He was making it possible for all people to be his people. Remember, that is what he wanted from the very beginning.

PRAYER   Close with prayer.

ASSIGNMENT   Encourage family members to make their own billboards. Encourage them to be creative and colorful. Have them share their work at the beginning of worship tomorrow.

 **Seventh Day (Tuesday)**

Light Four Purple Candles

The Fulfillment of the Promise to David

SCRIPTURE
READING

Luke 1:26-33

MATERIALS
NEEDED

A watch or clock with a moving second hand. A digital watch that denotes seconds will work as well. This object needs to be large enough for everyone to see.

LESSON

Light four purple candles. Call on a family member to read the Scripture for today.

Hold up the clock you have brought with you to worship. You might say, "I want you to sit perfectly still and watch two whole minutes go by. Don't move, don't talk, sit perfectly still for two minutes. Ready? Begin." Be sure to take part yourself.

DISCUSSION

After the two minutes have ended you might ask, "Did that two minutes seem like a long time? Was it hard to wait for the time to go by?" Allow each one to express his or her views. For most children two minutes of being perfectly still and quiet can seem like a lifetime. Continue by saying, "Two minutes does not sound like a long time, but while we are watching it pass, it seems very long! Imagine if we did the same thing for five minutes." (Allow for response.) Then ask them to imagine that we did the same thing for thirty minutes. (Allow again for response.)

"If two, or five, or thirty minutes is hard to wait and watch, just imagine how difficult it was for the people of Israel to wait for the Messiah. From the time of David to the birth of Jesus was roughly 900 years. That is 473 million minutes. Anyway you count it, that is a long time to wait. But wait they did. And God was faithful.

"When the time was right, God sent his Son to be the fulfillment of all the promises made to David. In Jesus, God established an eternal kingdom and reign through his Son over his people."

PRAYER

Close with prayer.

ASSIGNMENT

Ask everyone to think of different things people wait for. Encourage everyone to think of happy waiting (Christmas, Easter) and anxious waiting (family member in surgery, or on a long trip). Ask, "What is one thing we can do to make our waiting easier?" Tell everyone to be prepared to discuss how we wait at the next worship time.

The Promise of the Kingdom

INTRODUCTION TO
the Fifth Week of Lent

The idea of a "kingdom" is difficult for us to understand. A "kingdom" sounds like a place to us. That is why many people believe that "the kingdom of God," and "the kingdom of heaven" refer to our future home in heaven.

But the Bible uses the word *kingdom* in a special way. It does not necessarily mean "place." The word, as it is used in the Bible, means *the reign of God over his people*.

Because we live in a democracy and have no dealings with people who claim sovereign rule over us, we have difficulty understanding what a kingdom is. It is hard for us to imagine what living under a king's rule would be like. And yet, one of the most important promises God has made to us is that he will be our King and we will live in his kingdom.

The promise of the kingdom is to us God's offer of life. In God's kingdom we find his vision for community. In God's kingdom there is enough food for everyone; hunger is not allowed. In God's kingdom there are enough clothes for everyone, enough medicine, enough love. In God's kingdom there are no people who are better than other people. All people are equal before God and are equally loved and esteemed.

The promise of the kingdom is God's promise of a new creation, of a new humanity. In God's kingdom we are invited to live in the way he intended for us from the very beginning. The kingdom, of course, was fully embodied in the person and the preaching of Jesus. His first sermon dealt with the kingdom, and his teaching defined the meaning of the kingdom. Jesus' death was for the purpose of inaugurating the kingdom, and God raising Jesus from the dead was his own seal of approval on all that Jesus said and did about the kingdom.

For the next seven days we will explore the dimensions of this great and important promise.

 **First Day (Wednesday)**

Light Five Purple Candles

The Song of Kings

SCRIPTURE
READING

Psalm 2; Mark 1:11

MATERIALS
NEEDED

Make a banner that says "Happy Birthday." Allow the children to help, and let them guess whose birthday it is.

LESSON

Begin your worship time by lighting five purple candles. Point out that you are now beginning the fifth week of Lent. Remember, *lent* means preparation. Ask, "What are we preparing for?" (For Easter, the celebration of the Resurrection.)

Allow family members to report on their "waiting" assignment. Be sure to affirm everyone's effort.

Call on the designated family member to read Psalm 2. You will want to note especially verse 7. Also be prepared to read Mark 1:11. After the reading you might say something like, "In Israel, the crowning of a new king was a very important day. All the people would gather together, and the high priest would lead in a ceremony that confirmed the king. The psalm we read today is one of the songs the people of Israel would sing when a new king was crowned in their country."

DISCUSSION

Ask them to notice some of the special words used for king. In verse 2 the king is called the Lord's "anointed." Kings were called anointed because the priest would anoint them with oil, which was a symbol of the Holy Spirit. This was to indicate that God's own Spirit was "poured" out on this person.

In verse 6 he is simply called "king." But in verse 7 the psalmist tells us that God calls the new king "my son." All the kings in Israel were called "sons of God." This meant that they ruled with God's permission.

Notice that the psalm says, "Today I have begotten you." That means that no matter what family into which the king had been born, as of the day of his coronation, he was born as God's Son, God's new king. He was given a new birthday—the day of his birth as king over the people of Israel.

Read Mark 1:11 now. Notice that when Jesus was baptized, God called him his Son. Jesus was the only true King. He was King of kings. Jesus was always God's Son, and he was always God's chosen King. He was declared to be God's chosen King—chosen to bring to us the hope of the kingdom of God. God himself sang the song of the new King as Jesus was baptized and began his work for us.

As our king, Jesus can help us live the way God wants us to. Our job is to gladly follow him and trust him.

PRAYER   Close with prayer.

ASSIGNMENT   Ask family members to draw a picture that explains for them what it means for Jesus to be our king. This may be a baptism picture or a picture of Jesus receiving a crown. Be prepared to share the pictures as you worship together tomorrow.

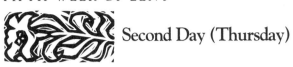 **Second Day (Thursday)**

Light Five Purple Candles

The Ideal Kingly Reign

SCRIPTURE READING	Isaiah 9:6-7
MATERIALS NEEDED	A globe or a large map of the world. If these are not available, a road map of part of the United States will work. What you are looking for is a way to imagine what our world looks like from outer space.
LESSON	Begin your worship time by lighting five purple candles. Call on a family member to read the passage from Isaiah.
DISCUSSION	After the reading, show everyone the map and say something like, "Imagine we are in a rocket, high above the earth. As we look down, we can see mountains and rivers; we can see forests and oceans. What we do not see are the problems. We cannot see pollution. We are unable to see hunger or crime. We are unable to see suffering and poverty. By being far enough away from the

earth we are able to imagine what the world would be like without these problems.

"In a way, that is what the prophet Isaiah did. He managed to get far enough away from his own situation to give us a picture of the ideal world." (Read verse 7 again.) Explain that the ideal world Isaiah saw was not from the distance of outer space. The ideal world he saw was in the future. God was promising that he would someday establish a kingdom that would bring peace and hope to our troubled world. Isaiah was able to look ahead and see that world.

"Jesus, of course, is the fulfillment of that promise. But wait! Jesus has come, and yet our world is not yet ideal. Our problems remain. How are we to understand this?

"The reason is that the ideal world is still in the future. But at least we know now how God will do it. The Lord will bring about healing in our world through Jesus Christ. The time will come when he will reign in peace."

Ask, "What are we to do in the meantime?" The answer is that we are to live as if he were already King. After all, in the lives of Christians, he is King.

PRAYER

Ask a family member to close your devotional time with prayer.

ASSIGNMENT   Allow family members to show their pictures of Jesus as King. Give everyone a chance to explain why they drew them the way they did. Tell everyone to draw another picture showing how Jesus as King will change the world. Be sure to put yourselves in the picture somewhere.

 **Third Day (Friday)**

Light Five Purple Candles

The Birth of the King

SCRIPTURE READING	Matthew 2:1-6
MATERIALS NEEDED	Cut a star out of cardboard. Cover it with tinfoil.
LESSON	Light five purple candles. Call on the designated family member to read the passage from Matthew. Take a moment to allow everyone to share his or her assignment from yesterday. Affirm your children as they grow forward in their understanding of the reign of God in their lives.

You might begin by saying, "It may seem funny to read a Christmas passage during Lent and Easter. We must remember, however, that Christmas does not make any sense without Easter. In other words, it is only because Jesus died and was raised from the dead that we celebrate Christmas in the first place."

DISCUSSION	Show everyone the star you have made. Pass it around and

let everyone hold it. Continue by saying, "Jesus was sent to the Jewish people as the fulfillment of the promises made to them in their Scriptures. But God wanted Jesus to be more than just King of the Jews. God wanted Jesus to be recognized as everybody's King. That is why he placed a special star in the heavens. This star was to let the world know that a new king was born. The promise of the kingdom was being offered to every person in the world."

Mention that the wise men who came to see Jesus, who followed the star, were probably not Jews. They knew about the Jewish Scriptures, enough to know a new king was to be born, but not enough to know how to find the new king.

There are many people in our world in the same situation. They believe God has some plan for them, but they don't know what that plan is. They don't know about the promise of Jesus and the kingdom. Ask, "What can we do?" We can be like God's star. We can tell others about the Easter promises and help them find Jesus just as the wise men found him.

The promises of the kingdom are important. These promises offer life and hope to all people. They were so important that God placed a special star in the heavens to light the way. Now he lights the way with our lives.

PRAYER   Close with prayer.

ASSIGNMENT   Ask everyone to think of at least two ways we can all be
                    "stars," helping people find their way to Jesus. Be prepared
                    to discuss these tomorrow.

 **Fourth Day (Saturday)**

Light Five Purple Candles

The Kingdom's Small Beginnings

SCRIPTURE
READING

Matthew 13:31-32

MATERIALS
NEEDED

A seed of some kind—an acorn, a kernel of corn, a dried bean, a flower seed—any of these will work.

LESSON

Light five candles. Be sure to caution little children from time to time not to ever light the candles without parents present. Call on the designated family member to read the passage from Matthew.

You might begin this worship time by saying something like the following. (Put this in your own words so that your feelings will be expressed.)

DISCUSSION

"We live in a difficult world. People suffer in our world, sometimes unfairly. There is hunger and poverty in many places. Children suffer and are frightened in our world. The picture of the ideal kingdom we read about the other night seems a million miles away from the reality of the world we live in. Occasionally I don't see how God can ever make his kingly presence known in such a difficult world."

Show everyone the seed you have brought. Continue by saying, "But then I remember that Jesus said the kingdom was like a mustard seed. A mustard seed was smaller than this seed. I think he meant two things by that."

Explain that one of the things Jesus meant when he said that the kingdom was like a mustard seed was that it starts small but grows into something big. That means the problems will not be solved all at once. God will gradually overtake them with his reign.

The second thing Jesus meant when he said that the kingdom was like a mustard seed was that the small things count. It's not just the rich and powerful who serve God in important ways. Regular people doing little things also help the kingdom grow.

Ask everyone to report at this time on the assignment from yesterday. Ask, "What two ways did everyone come up with to help people find their way to Jesus?" After everyone tells his or her ideas, continue by saying, "All of these are like mustard seeds. They are ways we help God make his reign known. God will pull all our efforts together with his own effort and bring about the ideal kingdom he has promised."

PRAYER   Close your worship time in prayer, thanking God for blessing the big and the small.

ASSIGNMENT   Encourage family members to select one of their ideas from yesterday and actually do it. Help little ones carry out their plan.

 **Fifth Day (Sunday)**

Light Five Purple Candles

Responding to the Kingdom

SCRIPTURE
READING

Matthew 13:44-46; Matthew 6:33

MATERIALS
NEEDED

Make a small poster that says, "Jesus Is the King of Kings."
Hide the poster somewhere in your house. Make a treasure
map that gives clues and directions to the map. For
instance, you could make the map in three or four parts.
Have the first part lead to other parts of the map. The final
part leads to the treasure. The treasure, of course, is that
Jesus is King of kings. Be creative and enthusiastic. Have
some fun with this.

LESSON

After the treasure hunt, light five candles and have a family member read the passages from Matthew.

You might begin by saying, "The Bible makes it clear
that finding the kingdom is the most important thing we
can do." Jesus said it was like a treasure. He also said we
should seek the kingdom above anything else we might
seek.

DISCUSSION

Ask, "But how do we do that? How do we seek the kingdom?" The treasure hunt will have given a clue. The answer is that we must seek the kingdom with all our energy. We must want it more than anything else. We must also seek the kingdom believing we will find it. It may be hidden, but it is not out of our reach. God has made himself available to all persons. We can find him if we try.

We must also seek the kingdom joyfully. Finding the kingdom is the key to living the way God wants us to. Pleasing God should fill us with a sense of great happiness.

PRAYER

Close your worship time by thanking God for the great treasure of his kingdom. Ask him to help us to live in his reign.

ASSIGNMENT

Ask everyone to make a list of all the reasons they can think of why the kingdom is important. Little ones may need help and may draw a picture of the blessings of the kingdom instead of a list.

 **Sixth Day (Monday)**

Light Five Purple Candles

Entering the Kingdom

SCRIPTURE
READING

Matthew 7:21-27

MATERIALS
NEEDED

Be prepared to play the game Simon Says. Give instructions, such as "Hold your hand in the air," but players
only do what they are instructed if you first say, "Simon
says."

LESSON

Light five purple candles. We are nearing the end of
this week. Remind everyone of the meaning of Lent. Call
on a family member to read the Scripture selection for
today.

Play the "Simon Says" game after the reading. After a few
minutes of play, switch the rules to "Jesus says." The point we
are working toward is this: Entering the kingdom requires
that we do what Jesus has instructed us to do.

Reread verse 21: "Not everyone who says to me 'Lord,
Lord,' shall enter the kingdom of heaven, but he who does
the will of my Father who is in heaven."

DISCUSSION

Take a moment and ask everyone to think of all the things they can remember that Jesus has told us to do. You may get responses cast in negative terms. Some of these are "don't lie, don't steal." Allow a few of these, but try to keep the focus on positive things the Lord has told us to do. Examples are, "love your neighbor," "pray," "practice forgiveness," and so forth.

After a few minutes of calling out ideas, play the "Jesus says," game again. This time use the ideas your family members have called out. For example, "Jesus says, 'Love your neighbor.'"

Here is an excellent time to explain the difference between "salvation by works," that is, the things we do, and "salvation by faith." Explain that we become God's children and are a part of the kingdom because we have done what Jesus said in believing in him as Savior. Because we are members of the kingdom, we now want to obey our King by doing the things he asks us to do.

Conclude your worship time by saying something like, "We are invited to enter God's kingdom, that is, to allow God to be our king. We are invited to join with Christ in bringing the world to an understanding of who Jesus is. We are invited to have peace in our lives and joy in our hearts. But there is only one way all of this can happen. We must ask him to be our Savior and our King. And because he is our King, we must obey him."

PRAYER   Close your worship time with prayer, thanking God for
             loving us enough to care how we live.

ASSIGNMENT   Encourage family members to think of other games we play
             that may be helpful in understanding God's work in our
             lives. For example, the game Old Maid can teach us the
             importance of planning ahead. The game Life can teach us
             about dealing with the unexpected. Even a game like domi-
             noes can teach us the importance of careful thinking and
             disciplined play.

 **Seventh Day (Tuesday)**

Light Five Purple Candles

The Fulfillment of the Kingdom

SCRIPTURE
READING

Matthew 28:18-20

MATERIALS
NEEDED

Draw a picture of a traffic light. On one side have the light red. On the other side have the light green.

LESSON

Light five purple candles. Ask a family member to read the Scripture passage for today.

After the reading, hold up the red light. You might say, "A light like this is used to help manage traffic. A red light means stop, and the green light means go."

DISCUSSION

Explain that, in one sense, with the life, death, and resurrection of Jesus, God has given us a green light. In fact, in the verses we read today, Jesus says plainly, "Go!" But why now? What now is different or new?

The new and different is simply that God has completed what he wanted to do for us. Everything we need is now in place. In the work of Jesus we have all the resources we need to fulfill God's plan. He wants to reign over a people dedicated and committed to him and his purposes.

That is what he wants—his own people. Ultimately, that is what the kingdom is about. In Christ, God has called out a new people. Ask, "What is our purpose? What does he want us to do?" The answer is shown in the verses read earlier: "Go, make disciples, teach, and baptize." God wants us to serve as a bridge over which people may cross and find him.

God has called us to be a servant people helping others find his love. That is the fulfillment of the kingdom. That is the reason we are here. That is the reason Jesus was raised from the dead. It is one of the key parts of the Easter promise.

PRAYER

Close your worship time in prayer asking God to help us "Go." Help us to understand we have a green light to offer the world his love.

ASSIGNMENT

Encourage family members to think of at least one person they each can tell about God's love. This person might be a family member or a friend. Little ones can be helped with this assignment. Notes or phone calls work very well.

The Promise of the Suffering Servant

INTRODUCTION TO
the Sixth Week of Lent

The early followers of Jesus were stunned by his death. They were certain that the Messiah would be a mighty ruler who would solve all their problems. These early Christians had been taught that the Hebrew Scriptures painted the Messiah in powerful, warlike images.

As they reflected on their experience of Jesus' resurrection, they realized that somehow they must have missed the point. The early church began a diligent search of the Hebrew Scriptures in an effort to find scriptural justification for a crucified Messiah. They were not disappointed.

Four poems or songs were discovered in Isaiah that seem to speak eloquently about the coming Messiah. These songs were originally thought to apply to Israel's suffering in Babylon. But as early Christians read them in the light of the Resurrection, it was clear that the character depicted in the songs was none other than Jesus, God's anointed.

Because the songs refer to this chosen person as "God's Servant," the poems have come to be called "The Suffering Servant Songs of Isaiah." They are among the most powerful and beautiful poetry in Hebrew and in English. These four poems will be the subject of our reflection and worship for the next four days. This short week ends on Palm Sunday. From there, we go to Holy Week—Jesus' last week on earth.

 **First Day (Wednesday)**

Light Six Purple Candles

Nothing Is to Be Wasted

SCRIPTURE READING	Isaiah 42:1-4
MATERIALS NEEDED	Arrange three or four sacks of assorted trash. If your family is already involved in recycling, use your own system. If not, this might be a good time to start. Separate plastic, paper, and metal into individual bags.
LESSON	Light six purple candles. Explain this is the sixth week of Lent. This will be a short week, only five nights. After Palm Sunday we begin Holy Week—the last week of Jesus' life. Call on a designated family member to read the Scripture passage from Isaiah. Use the introduction to this week to briefly explain the "Servant Songs."
	Take special notice of verse 3. Isaiah declares that the Suffering Servant will establish justice for the whole world. This means that not even a "dimly burning wick" or a "bruised reed" will be wasted.

These images refer to people. Some people barely seem to have enough energy to survive. The elderly might fall into this category. Others seem bruised and broken by life. Persons with addictions or other emotional problems might fall into this category. With God's servant, however, everyone is important, no one gets thrown away.

DISCUSSION

Point to the bags of trash you have brought. Say, "In our house there are some things we don't keep. We may recycle cans and newspapers, but we do not value them enough to keep them. We throw them away.

"Sadly, in our world, some people are so devalued that they get thrown away. The homeless, the hungry, the oppressed, and the powerless often fall into this category. These people are often the ones who end up on the trash heaps of life."

Explain that the Suffering Servant will be a king who will practice perfect justice and fairness. In his reign, and in his love, no one is wasted. No one is thrown away.

PRAYER

Close your worship time, thanking God for taking notice of even the most humble person in our world.

ASSIGNMENT

Try to determine if there are any hurting or needy people near where you live. Is there a nursing home nearby? Does your community have a rescue mission or soup kitchen? Is there a mentally handicapped intervention program in your area? All of these are places where we might find people whom some may consider as "useless." Discuss as a family how you might offer hope and love to one of these people.

 **Second Day (Thursday)**

Light Six Purple Candles

Called to Complete the Covenant

SCRIPTURE READING

Isaiah 49:1-6

MATERIALS NEEDED

A telephone. Also prepare a brief, make-believe conversation. Let the conversation be with someone who is performing some service or work for your family. Someone, for instance, might be painting a bedroom, or refinishing or reupholstering some furniture. (Be sure children understand this is a make-believe conversation.) The point you are trying to establish is that by overhearing your conversation with someone else, the family is able to learn what you are doing for them.

LESSON

Light six purple candles. Call on a family member to read the Servant Song from Isaiah 49:1-6. After the reading you might say, "Before we get started, I've got to make an important call." Pick up the telephone and perform your make-believe conversation.

   After you hang up, ask everyone, "What did you

overhear me saying? Was I talking to you? (No.) But I was talking about you."

DISCUSSION

Explain how the "Servant Song" read tonight has God doing something very similar. He is talking to the "coast-lands" (v. 1). These coastland areas were known as Gentile areas. The people of Israel did not have much love for Gentiles. But God was talking to these coastland areas about the Messiah who was to come. His purpose, of course, was for Israel to overhear his conversation and begin understanding the true purpose of his covenant promises.

From the very beginning, God wanted to call all people in the world to be his people. He invited Israel to be the first, but they were never intended to be his exclusive people. Through Israel God wanted to invite all of us to know him and love him.

The people of Israel had a hard time believing that. There were just some people they did not care for. Ask, "Are we like that? Are there people we don't care for?" Allow for response.

But God had a plan. He would send a servant king, who would someday rule over everybody, Jew and Gentile alike. "It is too light a thing," he says in verse 6, "to be just the servant to the people of Israel. You will be the Suffering

Servant king to the nations, to all people." That is the full hope of God's promise in Easter.

PRAYER

Close your worship time praying for people we may not care for, or people who frighten us or threaten us. Ask God to help us remember that all people are invited into his family.

ASSIGNMENT

Ask family members to make up a conversation between God and some of the people of the world. Pretend the people of your church overhear the conversation. What do you think God would say? How would the people in your church react? Work on this together as a family. Act it out when you finish.

 **Third Day (Friday)**

Light Six Purple Candles

Called to Be Beautiful

SCRIPTURE
READING

Isaiah 50:4-11

MATERIALS
NEEDED

Make a poster that says on one side "Taking the Pain," and on the other "Returning the Pain."

LESSON

Light six purple candles. Ask a family member to read the passage from the Servant Song for today.

You might begin by saying, "If someone hits us or tries to hurt us, our first response is to hit them back. In fact, it is very hard not to hit back. When someone hurts us, we want to give them hurt right back." (Hold up the poster with the side "returning the pain.")

"But Jesus was called to a different kind of work. He was called by God to be a Suffering Servant King. In this role, God asked him to take the pain we gave him." (Reread verses 6-7 again. Turn the poster over to the side that says, "Taking the Pain.")

DISCUSSION

Explain how Jesus was determined to perform faithfully what God asked him to do. What he was asked to do was very difficult. But the reward for his faithfulness was our salvation and redemption. Because Jesus was the faithful Suffering Servant, his life and death brought life for us. He took the pain and did not give it back. Instead, he gave back blessing and hope.

PRAYER

Close your worship time together expressing thanksgiving for Jesus' dedication and commitment to us. The love of God is nowhere more powerfully displayed than on the cross.

ASSIGNMENT

Ask family members to think of ways "taking the pain" might work with the people we have to deal with. Give children clear examples here. No child should be expected to take physical or mental abuse, especially from an adult, without doing something about it. However, among their friends and in their relationships with siblings, how might nonretaliation bring about peace? Help little ones find appropriate ways to apply this.

 **Fourth Day (Saturday)**

Light Six Purple Candles

Not a Likely Choice

SCRIPTURE READING	Isaiah 52:13–53:12
MATERIALS NEEDED	A plate of cookies or crackers. Be sure one cookie is covered with dirt or grass.
LESSON	Light six purple candles. Call on a family member to read the Scripture for today. After the reading you might say something like, "Before we get started tonight, I've brought some refreshments." Pass around the plate of cookies. Everyone, of course, will notice the cookie with the dirt on it. Say, "Oh well, I dropped that one. Just skip the dirty one and choose another."
DISCUSSION	After everyone has a cookie and the dirty one is left on the plate, you might say, "Wouldn't it be funny if this dirty cookie was a special, magic cookie, and whoever ate it would never be sick again? But no one will eat it because it looks dirty."

Tell the family that, in one way, that is what the Scripture reading is about. The Suffering Servant doesn't look like someone who could help us. When we get into trouble we want someone strong and mighty. But here is this servant who is beat up and killed.

But Isaiah says that his beating, his stripes, his wounds, heal us. Even though the Suffering Servant does not look like a good choice for our help and salvation, his servanthood saves us.

It makes us wonder if we have the wrong idea about what is really important and helpful in life.

PRAYER

Close your worship time in prayer, thanking God for sending an unlikely looking servant to die for our sins. We understand that through his death we are able to find life.

ASSIGNMENT

Ask the family to think of other ways we are fooled by the appearance of things. Think of toys that really looked like fun but turned out to be boring, or books that really looked interesting but were not good at all. How did you feel when your hopes were disappointed? Be prepared to discuss this tomorrow.

 **Fifth Day (Palm Sunday)**

Light Six Purple Candles

Praise for the Humble King

SCRIPTURE
READING

Matthew 21:1-9

MATERIALS
NEEDED

Palm branches or some other leafy branch. Try to provide enough for everyone to have one. If your community features any Palm Sunday activities such as a Palm Sunday processional, you might consider taking part with your family.

LESSON

Light six purple candles. Call on a family member to read the passage for today.

   After the reading distribute palm branches (or whatever) to everyone. You might say, "Today is Palm Sunday. We call this day Palm Sunday because as Jesus entered Jerusalem, the people laid their garments and leafy branches on the road to cushion his ride. More than likely, palm branches were used for this purpose."

DISCUSSION

Ask, "Why do you think they wanted to cushion the road Jesus was riding on?" Allow a few moments for response.

Continue by saying, "In the ancient world, kings and queens would travel through the streets of their city on carpets of cloth or even flowers. The people of Jerusalem laying their garments down for Jesus to ride on was their way of calling him their king. Notice what the people cried out as Jesus rode into Jerusalem: (read Matt. 21:9). These are titles used for the king of Israel."

Explain how there were some very strange things about this king. He did not ride a great white horse or in a golden chariot. Instead he rode on a young donkey's colt. He was not followed by his great army, but rather by a small group of disciples. Notice what Matthew says about all of this (read 21:5).

"Jesus did not ride into Jerusalem as a king triumphant, but rather as a servant king, a humble king. Jesus was fulfilling his role as the Suffering Servant of Israel (recall the past four days)."

"Look again at the palm branches in your hand. We are right to call Jesus King of kings and Lord of lords. But we must understand the kind of king he is. He is not a king who walks on soft carpet and sleeps in a plush palace. He is a servant king, a humble king. A Suffering Servant King goes to the lowly, the hurting, the broken. He identifies with the poor, the needy, the weak. A humble king welcomes children and offers relief for the weary and oppressed."

Ask, "Can we be glad that we have such a humble, servant king?" The answer, of course, is yes!

PRAYER   Close with prayer.

ASSIGNMENT   Churches that observe Lent and Easter celebrations every year often save their palm branches. When Ash Wednesday comes the next year, they take the palm branches from the previous year, burn them, and use the ashes to mark the forehead of their members with the sign of the cross. Get a large bag or envelope and save your palm branches for next year. Explain what you are doing so the family may look forward to next year's observance.

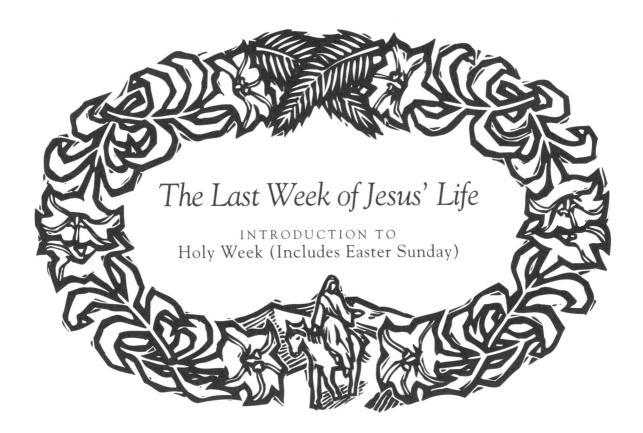

The Last Week of Jesus' Life

INTRODUCTION TO
Holy Week (Includes Easter Sunday)

Christians around the world mark Holy Week with special celebrations and ceremonies. Holy Week looks back to the last week of Jesus' earthly life.

Several important events took place during Holy Week that have helped us understand more clearly the Christian message. Also, the commitment of Jesus to be the Suffering Servant King reached an important climax during Holy Week.

As we begin this final week, we are going to modify what is known as a

"Tenebrae Service." The word *tenebrae* means darkness. Each day we will light seven candles. But each day we will extinguish one, then two, then three, and so on. By the time we reach Good Friday, we will light seven candles; then extinguish all but two. This gradual decreasing of light is meant to symbolize the darkness of the Cross.

We must ultimately face the terrible Cross. We must look into all of its darkness and horror. We must force ourselves to hear Jesus cry out in pain. We must stay there and watch as soldiers gamble for his only garment. We must stay there and watch him die.

Why? Why do we need to participate in all of the unpleasantness of the Cross? Why can't we simply skip over all of this and go straight to Easter?

The promises God made to his people through all the centuries were indeed fulfilled on the first Easter morning. But God's promises also include Good Friday—the day of crucifixion. Without the Cross there is no resurrection.

Light Seven Purple Candles
Extinguish One Candle

The Final Warning

SCRIPTURE
READING

John 12:27-38

MATERIALS
NEEDED

Make a large, colorful sign that says "Danger" or "Warning."

LESSON

Light seven purple candles, then extinguish one. Take a
moment and explain what the candles will symbolize this
final week (see introduction to Holy Week). Call on a family member to read John 12:27-38.

DISCUSSION

You might begin by saying, "It was very hard for the people
of Jerusalem to understand Jesus as a humble, servant king.
They were expecting their king to be a powerful king. That
is what is meant in verse 34—'Christ remains for ever!'
The promises of God were fulfilled through a suffering
king. The people of Israel were stunned.

"But Jesus tried to warn them. (Hold up your Danger
sign.) Over and over again he told them, 'The Son of

man must suffer' (Mark 8:31) and be 'lifted up from the earth' (John 12:32). In our reading for today, God himself even speaks from heaven as a final warning. This was the beginning of the final week. Jesus would not be with them much longer. He tried in vain to help them understand.

"The people of Israel had the wrong idea about their coming king. They wanted someone strong and powerful. What they got was a suffering servant. As a humble servant, Jesus was able to draw all persons to himself. That is the wisdom and greatness of God's plan."

PRAYER

Close your worship time, thanking God for his gentleness and kindness. Thank him also for sending us a king who gave his life that we might live.

ASSIGNMENT

Ask the younger ones in the family to draw a picture of God warning the people of Israel not to misunderstand his Son. Ask older children to make a list of the ways people misunderstand Jesus today. If Jesus is a suffering servant, where is he right now?

Light Seven Purple Candles
Extinguish Two Candles

Anointed by Mary

SCRIPTURE
READING

Mark 14:1-9

MATERIALS
NEEDED

A bottle of perfume or cologne. If you happen to have some expensive French perfume, you might want to use it for this lesson.

LESSON

Light seven purple candles; extinguish two of them. Call on the designated family member to read the Scripture for today.

After the reading, show everyone the perfume or cologne bottle. You might say, "This is very expensive perfume. We would not want to waste it. In the time of Jesus, sometimes on special occasions, someone might, during a party or dinner, pour such perfume on a special guest, in somewhat the same way we surprise someone with a birthday party. Also, when a person died, the body was carefully washed and covered with perfume before it was buried. In the case of some poor families, the perfume needed to anoint a beloved family member was often their most treasured possession, sometimes their only possession. They would certainly not want to waste it.

"The Gospel of John (12:1-3) tells us the woman was Mary, sister of Martha and Lazarus. Not only was the perfume costly in terms of its worth, but it was also an intensely personal gift."

DISCUSSION

Ask the members of the family why they think Mary did this. What motivated her to perform such an elaborate and expensive act? Jesus said it was an anointing for his own burial. In other words, her act of love and generosity was a way of showing gratitude for what Jesus had done for her. Perhaps Mary was also feeling sadness and sorrow for what Jesus was about to go through.

Point out that as we move toward Easter it is not unusual for us to experience feelings of sadness and regret. The thought of Jesus suffering and dying on the cross is not an easy scene for us to imagine. And when we realize it was for us that he died, our sorrow only grows.

But sadness is not the only feeling we may have. Like Mary, who anointed Jesus, we may also feel thankful. God made a promise to all people. He would bless them and make them his people. Jesus' death on the cross was the way God kept that promise.

PRAYER

Close your worship time in silence. Encourage everyone to express silently to God their feelings about Jesus' death.

ASSIGNMENT

Encourage family members to think of ways we can express thanks to God for what Jesus has done. We can say thank you, and we should. But is there anything we can do? Encourage everyone to be prepared to give at least one idea tomorrow.

Light Seven Purple Candles
Extinguish Three Candles

Betrayed by His Friends

SCRIPTURE
READING

Matthew 26:14-25

MATERIALS
NEEDED

Paper and crayons or pencils

LESSON

Light all seven purple candles. Then extinguish three of them. Remind everyone of the meaning of the candles. As Jesus neared the Cross, the world slipped into gradual, growing darkness. Call on a family member to read the Scripture. After the reading call for reports from yesterday's assignment.

Distribute paper and pencils or crayons. Ask everyone to either write the name of his or her best friend or draw a picture of that best friend (for those little ones who are not yet able to write). Ask family members to tell the name of the best friend and one thing that makes that friend special. (Note: Little ones may want to name "Jesus" as their best friend, which is wonderful. But for this lesson encourage them to name flesh-and-blood friends.)

DISCUSSION

After each one has told about his or her friend, you might say, "Imagine how we would feel if our best friend did something to hurt us. How would you feel if your friend did something really mean to you?" Allow everyone a chance to answer.

Explain that during the last week of Jesus' life, one of his best friends did something terrible. Judas led the enemies of Jesus to his secret resting place in a garden near Gethsemane. They were able to arrest Jesus there only because Judas showed them the way and pointed Jesus out with a kiss.

Ask, "Why did Judas do this?" No one knows for sure. Maybe it was for money. Maybe he was angry with Jesus about something. But this much we do know. It hurts to be betrayed by a friend. As Jesus made his way to the Cross, he had to carry the deep disappointment that one of his own friends became an enemy.

PRAYER

Close your worship time asking God to help us always be faithful friends to those who trust us and love us.

ASSIGNMENT

Ask family members to take another look at the name (or picture) of their best friend. Ask, "Does this person know how special he is to you? Have you been a good friend to him? Maybe you should call your friend before tomorrow night and tell him how much you love him."

 **MAUNDY THURSDAY**

Light Seven Purple Candles
Extinguish Four Candles

The Giving of the New Covenant

SCRIPTURE READING	Matthew 26:26-29
MATERIALS NEEDED	A cup of grape juice and a whole, uncut loaf of bread.*
LESSON	Light all seven purple candles. Extinguish four of them. Call on a family member to read the Scripture.

After the reading you might begin by saying, "God made several covenants. The first one, however, was the promise made to Abraham. Remember the promise made to Abraham? God promised that through Abraham all the world would be blessed. Jesus, as we know, is the fulfillment of that promise."

*If you are part of a Christian tradition that teaches that the Eucharist (Lord's Supper) may only be administered by a priest, please feel free to modify this lesson so that the juice and bread are object lessons only. I encourage you to attend a Maundy Thursday service so that the lesson might become real through participation. Persons who are part of the Protestant evangelical tradition, who accept the idea of the priesthood of all believers, may freely lead their families in a celebration of the Lord's Supper.

DISCUSSION

Point out that on the night Jesus was arrested, he took time to have a final supper with his disciples. He used part of the meal to help his friends understand that the new covenant was finally theirs—the promise was being kept.

First, Jesus took a loaf of bread and blessed it. Then he passed the loaf around, and each disciple broke off a piece. Jesus said, "Take, eat; this is my body."

Hold up the loaf of bread. Pray a short prayer. Thank God for giving his Son to us. After the prayer, break the loaf and give each family member a piece. Take one yourself. Say, "Jesus said this bread represented his body. We eat this bread to remember what our Lord has done." Eat the bread.

Continue by saying, "Jesus also took a cup of wine and blessed it. He said, 'Drink of it, all of you; for this is my blood of the covenant.' Then Jesus passed the cup around for all the disciples to share."

Hold up the cup of grape juice. Offer a short prayer. After the prayer you might say, "This cup represents the fulfillment of God's covenant by the sacrifice of Jesus. We drink from this cup to remember how much he loves us." Drink from the cup and pass it to every family member.

PRAYER

Close your worship time together holding hands and singing a favorite hymn or simply enjoying the presence of God together.

ASSIGNMENT   Ask family members to think carefully about the bread and the juice. Ask them to be ready to tell how they felt about the experience.

 GOOD FRIDAY

Light Seven Purple Candles
Extinguish Five Candles

"It Is Finished"

SCRIPTURE READING	John 19:23-30
MATERIALS NEEDED	Make a cross out of small boards or sticks. Locate three large nails.
LESSON	Light all seven purple candles. After they are burning extinguish five of them. Have a designated family member read the Scripture for today.

Take a moment to explain where the expression Good Friday comes from. Little ones may find it difficult to accept that the Friday Jesus died was a "good" Friday.

The day, of course, was terrible. Show everyone the cross and nails. Our Lord died for our sins. But it was for our good that he died. He died willingly to save us. Ask, "What is it that makes Good Friday good?" Allow everyone to struggle with the question. Affirm all responses.

DISCUSSION

Continue by saying, "Good Friday became good on Easter Sunday! Death did not defeat Jesus. God raised him from the dead, and he lives forever to help us."

Call attention to Jesus' words from the reading. John 19:30 says that Jesus cried out "'It is finished:' and he bowed his head and gave up his spirit." Ask, "What do you think Jesus meant when he said, 'It is finished?'" Encourage them to think of as many ideas as they can.

When Jesus said, "It is finished," he was saying, "It is all done. The promises are all kept. Everything that people need, to become the people of God, is now in place. I have done what I came to do. My work here is finished." And with those words on his lips, he died.

PRAYER

Close your worship time looking closely at the two candles burning. The world looked very dark to Jesus' friends. Our world also appears dark at times. Pray for our troubled world.

ASSIGNMENT

Ask everyone to draw a picture of Jesus on the cross. On the ground below the cross show the different people who watched Jesus die. Somewhere in the crowd, draw yourself. Ask, "How would it have felt to have been there?"

Light Seven Purple Candles
Extinguish Six Candles

"As Secure As You Can"

SCRIPTURE
READING

Matthew 27:62-66

MATERIALS
NEEDED

A lock with its key

LESSON

Light all seven purple candles. After they are all burning, extinguish all but one. One lone candle lights our wait for Easter. The death of Jesus seemed like the end. For a moment it seemed as if darkness would win after all.

Call on a family member to read the Scripture passage assigned for today. After the reading you might explain the background briefly.

Jesus' enemies had heard he was supposed to be raised from the dead. They did not believe it. They thought his disciples would attempt to steal the body and claim he was resurrected. These enemies of Jesus explained their suspicion to Pilate, the Roman governor. He posted a guard around the tomb and told the enemies of Jesus, "Make the tomb as secure as you can."

Their efforts, however, were a complete waste of time. No power in this world could stand against God's power to overcome death.

DISCUSSION

Show everyone the lock and key. You might say, "It was easy for God to raise Jesus from the dead. Death could not stop him, the Roman guards could not stop him, the seal on the stone could not stop him." Take the key and unlock the lock. Say, "Just as it is easy for me to unlock this lock, so it is easy for God to unlock death and raise his Son back to life."

Explain how they made the tomb as secure as they could. They very much wanted Jesus to stay in there and stay dead. But their puny strength was no match for God's power. He was determined to raise Jesus from the dead, and early on the first Easter morning he did!

PRAYER

Close your worship time, thanking God for using his great power to defeat death in our world and in our lives.

ASSIGNMENT

Tomorrow is Easter morning. Your family may have a regular tradition of attending a sunrise service or enjoying an early Easter breakfast. Agree together as a family to set the first light of Easter aside to worship together. Remind everyone that our goal is to deepen our appreciation for what God has done for us in raising Jesus from the dead.

 **EASTER**

Light Seven Purple Candles
Light One Large White Candle

He Is Risen!

SCRIPTURE
READING

Matthew 28:1-10

MATERIALS
NEEDED

Try to make the room where you are worshiping as dark as possible. If you are meeting early Easter morning, try to get started before the first light. Allow only the candles to light the room.

LESSON

Light all seven purple candles. Add one large white candle. You might want to arrange the purple candles in a circle (if they are free-standing). Otherwise, simply place the white candle in a prominent place among the others. Call on a family member to read the Easter account from Matthew.

Be prepared to tell with some feeling the following paraphrase of the first Easter experience.

"The morning air was cool and crisp as the women made their way to the tomb. They had not slept at all. They were tired, and they were heartbroken. Their beloved Jesus had been executed by the Romans. It all happened so fast that they had not been able to properly prepare his body. That was the purpose of their early morning journey.

"As they arrived at the tomb, however, they were shocked to see the stone already moved away. As they looked inside, they could not believe their eyes. The tomb was empty.

"Suddenly an angel appeared. He spoke to them the most wonderful words they had ever heard. 'He is not here. He is risen!' In their wildest dreams they did not believe God would raise Jesus. But he did."

DISCUSSION

Ask your family members this question: "Why is the resurrection of Jesus so important?" Allow everyone a chance to respond.

To answer the question, explain that the Resurrection is important for several reasons:

1. It was God's way of saying Jesus was right. Everything Jesus said and did was true. It shows that God had accepted Jesus' sacrifice for our sins.

2. The Resurrection also makes it possible for Jesus to continue to be with us. His Spirit is now in everyone who believes in him.

3. The Resurrection is also God's way of keeping all of his promises. He invites us to be his children, and in return he blesses us with eternal life. We know he can give us this blessing because of the Resurrection.

That is the great promise of Easter. In a world of death and darkness, God has shown his power to defeat death and darkness. We need not fear death. We are God's people, his children. He has blessed us and given us his Son. He has kept all his promises. And Easter is the greatest of them all.

PRAYER

Close your family worship time with a prayer of thanksgiving. Praise God for his gracious acts of kindness. Thank God for defeating death and giving us life. Praise God for sending his Son. Ask God to help us live our lives free of darkness and always live in the light of Easter.

ASSIGNMENT

Spend the day celebrating the gift God has given us in his Son.

May the Lord richly bless you and your family as you serve in his name.

Imaginative, Practical Resources for Home and Family—from Tyndale House

Also by James Evans:
FAMILY DEVOTIONS FOR THE ADVENT SEASON 0-8423-0865-2

THE BIG BOOK OF GREAT GIFT IDEAS 0-8423-1148-3
GREAT CHRISTMAS IDEAS
0-8423-1056-8
Alice Chapin

FAMILY TRADITIONS THAT LAST A LIFETIME
Karen M. Ball and Karen L. Tornberg
0-8423-1371-0

THE IDEA BOOK FOR MOTHERS
Pat Hershey Owen 0-8423-1558-6

THE ONE YEAR BIBLE MEMORY BOOK FOR FAMILIES
David R. Veerman 0-8423-1387-7

THE WELCOMING HEARTH
Elizabeth R. Skoglund 0-8423-7919-3

THE FAMILY DEVOTIONS BIBLE
This fantastic Bible teaches key biblical values through easy-to-use devotionals, positioned right next to the Scriptures on which they are based. Available in *The Living Bible* verson, hardcover and softcover.